Bible Stories for Children

The New Testament

Kent Burke

THIS BOOK BELONGS TO:_____

Another fine book from the Light and The Way Press

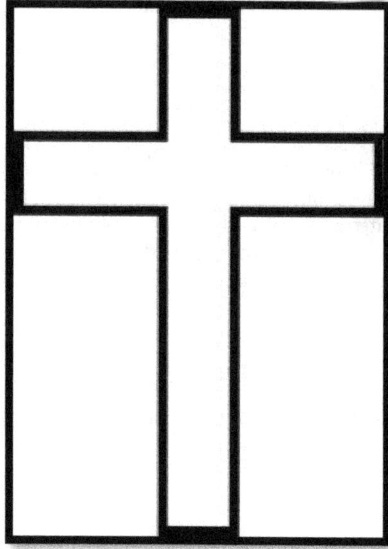

An imprint of LLR Books

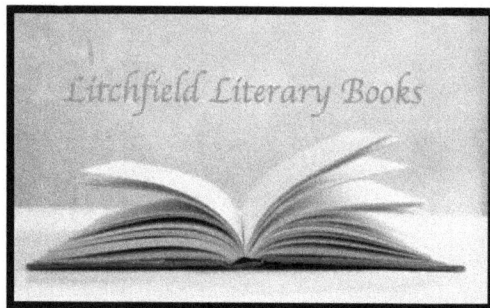

Visit our Web site: WWW. Litchfield Literary Books.Com

PREFACE

"The Children's Bible" provides, in simple English, a translation of selections from both the Old and the New Testament. These selections have been made as a result of more than twenty-five years of observation and study. The text is that of the Bible itself, but in the language of the child, so that it may easily be read to the younger children and by those who are older. It is not in words of one syllable, for while the child is reading the Bible he should gradually learn the meaning of new words and idioms.

The Bible contains the foundations on which the religious life of the child must be built. The immortal stories and songs of the Old and NewTestaments are his richest inheritance from the past. To give him this heritage in language and form that he can understand and enjoy is the duty and privilege of his parents and teachers.

It is hoped that "The Children's Bible" will meet the need and the demand, which parents and educators alike have long felt and often expressed, for a simple translation of selections from the Bible most suited to the needs and the interests of the child. It is also believed that after the child has learned to appreciate and love these stories and songs, he will be eager and able to read the Bible as a whole with genuine interest and understanding.

INDEX

JESUS IS BORN AT BETHLEHEM

The angel Gabriel was sent from God to a young woman named Mary in Nazareth, a town of Galilee. She was to be married to a man named Joseph of the family of David. When he came to her the angel said: "Hail, highly honored one! God is with you!"

She was startled by his words and wondered what such a greeting might mean. But the angel said to her, "Fear not, Mary, for you have found favor with God. You will have a son and will name him Jesus. He will be great and will be called the Son of the Most High."

Then Mary said to the angel, "How can this be, for I am not yet married." The angel answered her, "The Holy Spirit will come upon you and the power of the Most High will cover you; therefore your child will be called holy, the Son of God." Mary said: "I am God's servant. May it be with me as you say." Then the angel left her.

In those days the Emperor Augustus commanded that every one should be registered. So all went to be registered, each to his own town. Joseph, because he was of the family of David, went to be registered with Mary, his wife, from the town of Nazareth in Galilee to Bethlehem in Judea where David was born. While they were there Mary's first son was born. And she wrapped him in swaddling-clothes and laid him in a manger, because there was no room for them in the inn.

In that country there were shepherds living in the fields and keeping watch over their flocks by night. And an angel from God stood by themand a heavenly light shone around them, and they were frightened. But the angel said to them:

"Fear not, for behold I bring you good news
Of great joy which shall be for all the people.
For to you is born this day in the town of David
A Saviour who is God's Anointed.
This will be a sign to guide you:
You will find a baby in swaddling-clothes lying in a manger."

Then suddenly there was with the angel a great number of the heavenly ones singing praise to God and saying:

"Glory to God on high,
And on earth peace, good-will among men."

When the angels had gone away from them into heaven, the shepherds said to one another, "Let us go now to Bethlehem to see this which God has made known to us." So they went quickly and found Mary and Joseph; and the baby was lying in a manger.

When they had seen him, they made known what had been told them about this child. All who heard the words of the shepherds wondered, but Mary kept these things to herself and often thought about them. And the shepherds returned, thanking and praising God for what they had heard and seen, as it had been foretold.

THE WISE MEN BRING GIFTS TO THE YOUNG CHILD

When Jesus was born in Bethlehem, wise men from the east came to Jerusalem and asked, "Where is the newly born King of the Jews? For we saw his star in the east and have come to worship him."

When Herod heard these things, he and every one else in Jerusalem were greatly troubled. So when he had gathered all the high priests and scribes together, he asked them where the Christ was to be born. They said to him, "In Bethlehem of Judea."

Then Herod privately called the wise men and asked them exactly how long the star had been seen since it appeared in the east. And he sent them to Bethlehem with the command, "Go and search carefully for the young child, and when you have found him, come and let me know, that I also may go and worship him." When they had heard the king, they went away, and the star which they had seen in the east went before them until it stood over the place where the young child was. They were overjoyed at the sight; and when they came into the house and saw the child with Mary, his mother, they knelt down and worshipped him. Opening their treasures they presented to him gifts of gold, frankincense and myrrh. But being warned in a dream not to return to Herod, they went back to their own country by another way.

THE BOY JESUS ASKS QUESTIONS

After Joseph and Mary had done all that the law commanded, they returned to Galilee to their own town of Nazareth. And the boy Jesus grew and became strong in body and mind. And the blessing of God was upon him.

Now his parents went every year to Jerusalem to the Feast of the Passover, and when he was twelve years old they went up as usual. After they had stayed the full number of days and were returning, the boy Jesus remained behind in Jerusalem. His parents did not know this; but, supposing him to be in the caravan, they travelled on for a whole day. Then they searched for him among their relatives and friends. When they did not find him, they returned to Jerusalem, still looking for him. After three days they found him in the Temple, sitting with the teachers, listening to them and asking them questions. All who heard him were amazed at his intelligence and his answers.

When his parents saw him, they were astonished; and his mother said to him, "Son, why have you treated us like this? Your father and I have been anxiously looking for you." He said to them, "Why did you look for me? Did you not know that I must be in my Father's house?" But they did not understand what he meant.

Then he went down with them and came to Nazareth; and he was obedient to them; but his mother kept all these sayings in her heart. And Jesus grew in wisdom and body and in favor with God and man.

JOHN THE BAPTIST TELLS OF JESUS' WORK

While Pontius Pilate was governor of Judea and Herod was ruler of Galilee, a man named John, the son of Zachariah, lived in the desert country. And God commanded him and he went into all the country around the river Jordan calling upon men to be baptized to show that they were sorry for their sins and wished to be forgiven. Those who were truly sorry for their sins, he baptized in the river Jordan. This John wore a garment of camel's hair and a leather belt, and his food was locusts and wild honey.

Then the people of Jerusalem and all Judea and the country around the Jordan began to go out to him to confess their sins and to be baptized by him in the Jordan.

To the crowds that went out to be baptized by him he said, "You children of vipers! Who warned you to flee from the coming wrath? Bear fruits, then, that will prove that you are truly sorry for what you have done. Do not say to yourselves, 'We are children of Abraham'; for I tell you, God can raise up children for Abraham from these stones. Already the axe lies at the root of the trees. Every tree, therefore, that does not bear good fruit is cut down and thrown into the fire."

The crowds kept asking him, "What must we do?" He answered them, "Let him who has two coats share with him who has none; and let him who has food do the same."

When the tax-gatherers came to be baptized, they said to him, "Teacher, what must we do?" He said to them, "Do not take more from any one than rightfully belongs to you." Soldiers also asked him, "And what must we do?" To them he said, "Do not take money from anybody by force, nor make false charges, but be content with your wages."

Now as the people were wondering whether John might possibly be the Christ, John said to them all, "I indeed baptize you with water; but One is coming mightier than I, whose shoe-strings I am not worthy to untie. He will baptize you with the Holy Spirit and with fire. His fan is in his hand, and he will thoroughly cleanse his threshing-floor, and will gather the wheat into his storehouse; but the chaff he will burn up with fire that cannot be put out." In this way, and with many other earnest words, he told the good news to the people.

JESUS DECIDES HOW HE WILL DO HIS WORK

At this time Jesus came from Nazareth in Galilee and was baptized by John in the Jordan. And as he was coming up from the water, he saw the heavens opening and the Spirit, like a dove, coming down upon him. And a voice from heaven said,

> "Thou art my beloved Son,
> In thee I am well pleased."

Then Jesus was led by the Spirit into the wilderness to be tempted by the devil. And after he had fasted forty days and forty nights he was hungry. Then the tempter came and said to him, "If you are the Son of God, command these stones to become bread." But Jesus answered, "It is written,

> "'Man is not to live on bread alone,
> But on every word that comes from God.'"

Then the devil took him to the holy city and, setting him on the highest point of the Temple, said to him, "If you are the Son of God, throw yourself down; for it is written,

> "'He will give his angels charge of you,
> And on their hands they will bear you up,
> Lest you strike your foot against a stone.'"

Jesus said to him, "It is also written,

"'You shall not tempt the Lord your God.'"

Once more the devil took him to a high mountain and showed him all the kingdoms of the world and their glory, and he said to him, "All these things I will give you if you will fall down and worship me." Jesus said to him, "Away with you, Satan! for it is written,

"'You shall worship the Lord your God,
And him only shall you serve.'"

JESUS WINS DEVOTED FRIENDS

Herod seized John the Baptist and bound him, and put him in prison because of Herodias, his brother Philip's wife, for John said to him, "It is not right for you to have her." And although Herod wanted to put him to death, he was afraid of the people, for they believed John to be a prophet.

Now after John was put in prison, Jesus came into Galilee, preaching God's good news: "The time has come; repent of your sins and believe in the good news, for the kingdom of God is at hand."

Leaving Nazareth, Jesus went to live in Capernaum, which is on the Sea of Galilee. As he was passing along the shore of the Sea of Galilee, he saw Simon and Andrew his brother casting their nets into the sea, for they were fishermen.

Jesus said to them, "Come with me, and I will make you fishers of men." And they at once left their nets and followed him. And going a little farther on, he saw James, the son of Zebedee, with John his brother, who were in their boat mending their nets. He called them, and they at once left their father, Zebedee, in the boat with the hired men, and went with him.

Then Jesus found Philip and said to him, "Come with me."

Now Philip was from Bethsaida, the home of Andrew and Peter. Philip, finding Nathanael, said to him, "We have found him of whom Moses in the law and also the prophets wrote: Jesus of Nazareth, the son of Joseph." But Nathanael said to him, "Can anything good come out of Nazareth?" Philip replied, "Come and see."

Jesus saw Nathanael coming to him and said to him, "Here is a true Israelite, in whom there is no deceit."

Nathanael said to him, "How do you know me?" Jesus answered, "Before Philip called you, when you were under the fig-tree, I saw you."

Nathanael answered him, "Rabbi, you are the Son of God, you are the King of Israel." Jesus replied, "Do you believe because I said to you, 'I saw you under the fig-tree'? You shall see greater things than these!"

THE WEDDING AT CANA

Two days later there was a wedding at Cana in Galilee; and the mother of Jesus was there. Jesus and his disciples had also been invited. When the wine had all been used, Jesus' mother said to him, "They have no wine."

Jesus answered, "What is that to me? My time has not yet come."

His mother said to the servants, "Do whatever he tells you." Six stone water-jars (such as the Jews used in washing) were there; each jar would hold about twenty gallons. Jesus said, "Fill up the jars with water."

So they filled them to the brim. Then Jesus said, "Pour some out, and take it to the one in charge of the feast." And they did so. When the one in charge of the feast tasted the water which had become wine, he did not know where it came from (although the servants who had poured out the water knew), so he called the bridegroom and said to him, "Every one serves the good wine first, and the wine that is not so good after men have drunk freely; but you have kept the good wine until now." This the first of his wonderful signs, showing his power, Jesus did at Cana in Galilee; and his disciples believed in him.

THE HEALING OF THE TEN LEPERS

On their way to Jerusalem, Jesus and his disciples passed through Samaria and Galilee. When he entered a certain village, he was met by ten lepers, who cried to him from a distance, "Jesus, Master, have pity on us."

When Jesus saw them he said to them, "Go, and show yourselves to the priests." And as they went, they were made clean.

One of them, when he saw that he was healed, turned back, and with a loud voice praised God; and he fell down at the feet of Jesus with his face to the ground and thanked him; and this man was a Samaritan.

Jesus said to him, "Were not ten made clean? Where are the other nine? Was there no one who returned to give praise to God except this stranger?"

And Jesus said to him, "Arise, and go on your way, your faith has made you well."

HEALING THE MAN AT THE POOL

There was a festival of the Jews in Jerusalem, and Jesus went there. In Jerusalem there is a pool beside the sheep gate. In Hebrew it is called, Bethesda. It has five porches, and a crowd of people who were sick, blind, lame or helpless were lying there, waiting for the water to move, for an angel of the Lord went down into the pool at certain times and stirred the water; and the first person who stepped into the water after it was stirred was made well, no matter what disease he had.

One man was there who had been ill for thirty-eight years. Jesus saw him lying there, and knew that he had been ill for a long time; and he said to him, "Do you want to be made well?"

The sick man answered, "Sir, I have no one to put me in the pool when the water is stirred, and while I am getting in, some one else steps in before me."

Jesus said to him, "Arise, take up your bed, and walk." Immediately the man was made well, and he took up his bed and walked.

JESUS TALKS WITH A SAMARITAN WOMAN

When Jesus left Judea and went back into Galilee, he had to pass through Samaria; and he came to a city of Samaria called Sychar, near the piece of ground that Jacob gave his son Joseph. Now Jacob's well was there. Jesus, therefore, being wearied by the journey, sat down by the well. It was about noon and a woman of Samaria came to draw water. Jesus said to her, "Give me a drink." (For his disciples had gone away into the city to buy food.)

The Samaritan woman said to him, "How is it that you, a Jew, ask a drink of me who am a Samaritan?" for the Jews have nothing to do with Samaritans. Jesus answered her, "If you knew the gift of God and who it is who says to you, 'Give me a drink,' you would have asked him and he would have given you living water." The woman said to him, "Sir, you have nothing with which to draw and the well is deep; where then do you get that living water? Are you greater than our father Jacob who gave us the well and himself drank from it, together with his children and his cattle?"

Jesus answered her, "Whoever drinks of this water will thirst again; but whoever drinks of the water that I will give shall never thirst. The water that I give him will become in him a well of water springing up into eternal life." The woman said to him, "Sir, give me this water, that I may not thirst again nor have to come here to draw."

Jesus said to her, "Go, call your husband, then come back here." The woman answered, "I have no husband." Jesus said to her, "You are right in saying, 'I have no husband,' for you have had five husbands, and he whom you now have is not your husband; in saying that, you spoke the truth."

The woman said to him, "Sir, I see that you are a prophet. Our fathers worshipped in this mountain; and you Jews say that Jerusalem is the place where men ought to worship." Jesus said to her, "Woman, believe me, the time will come when you will worship the Father neither on this mountain nor at Jerusalem. The time is coming, yes, has already come, when the true worshippers will worship the Father in spirit and in truth; for such worshippers the Father seeks. God is a spirit, and they who worship him must worship him in spirit and in truth." The woman said to him, "I know that the Messiah (which means Christ) is coming. When he comes he will explain all things to us." Jesus said to her, "I who am talking to you am he."

At this point the disciples came up and were astonished that he was talking with a woman; but none of them said, "What do you want?" or, "Why are you talking to her?"

Then the woman left her water-pot and going into the city said to the men, "Come, see a man who told me all that I ever did. Is not this the Messiah?" And they set out from the town on their way to him.

Meanwhile Jesus' disciples urged him, saying, "Master, take some food"; but he said to them, "I have food to eat of which you know not." So they said to one another, "Has any one brought him something to eat?" Jesus said to them, "My food is to do the will of him who sent me and to carry out his work. Do not say, 'Four months and then comes the harvest'; I say to you, lift up your eyes and see these fields white for the harvest! Already the reaper is receiving his wages and gathering in a crop for eternal life, that the sower and reaper may rejoice together. For here the proverb holds true, 'One sows and another reaps.' I sent you to reap a harvest for which you had not toiled; other men have toiled and you are sharing the results of their toil."

Because of the words of the woman who had said, "He told me everything that I ever did," many Samaritans from the town believed in Jesus; and when they came to him, they begged him to stay with them. And he stayed there two days, and many more believed because of what he himself said. To the woman they said, "Now we believe, not because of your words but because we have heard for ourselves and know that this is indeed the Saviour of the world."

GIVING LIFE TO A WIDOW'S SON

Jesus went to a town called Nain; and his disciples went with him followed by a large crowd. Just as Jesus came to the gate of the town, he saw one who was dead being carried out. He was the only son of his mother who was a widow. Many people of the town were with her.

When Jesus saw her, he had sympathy for her and said to her, "Do not weep." And he came and touched the coffin, and those who carried it stood still. Jesus said: "Young man, I say to you, arise."

And he who had been dead sat up and began to speak. And Jesus gave him back to his mother. And all the people were filled with fear and praised God, saying, "

A great prophet has appeared among us, and God has visited his people." And the story of what Jesus had done was told in all of Judea and the country around there.

JESUS HEALS THE SICK

Jesus and his disciples entered Capernaum; and on the next Sabbath he went into the synagogue and began to teach. And the people were astonished at his teaching, for he taught them as one who had authority, and not as the scribes.

In their synagogue that day was a man under the power of an unclean spirit, who cried out, "What have you to do with us, Jesus of Nazareth? Have you come to destroy us? I know you are God's Holy One."

But Jesus reproved the unclean spirit, saying, "Be still, and come out of him." Then the unclean spirit, after convulsing the man, came out of him with a loud cry. The people were so astonished that they began to ask one another, "What is this? Is it a new teaching? With authority he commands even the unclean spirits and they obey him." So the news about Jesus spread at once in every direction all through the country about Galilee.

After leaving the synagogue they went straight to the house of Simon and Andrew; and James and John went with them. The mother of Simon's wife was ill in bed with a fever; so at once they told Jesus about her. He went to her and, taking her by the hand, lifted her up. Then the fever left her, and she began to wait upon them.

In the evening, after the sun had set, they brought to him all who were sick or under the control of evil spirits, until all the people of the city were gathered at the door. He healed many who were sick with different kinds of diseases, and cast out many evil spirits, but would not let them speak, because they knew who he was.

One day a leper came to him and on bended knees begged him: "If you will, you can make me clean." Feeling sorry for him, Jesus stretched out his hand and touched him, and said, "I will; be cleansed!" At once the leprosy left him and he was cleansed. Then Jesus, after strictly warning him, sent him away with the command, "See that you do not say a word to any one, but go, show yourself to the priest and offer what Moses commanded as proof to them that you are clean." But the man went away and began to tell every one about it, so that Jesus could no longer enter a city openly, but had to stay outside in lonely places; and people from everywhere came to him.

JESUS CURES A MAN WHO CANNOT WALK

When Jesus entered Capernaum again, after some days, it was reported that he was at home, and so many people gathered about him that there was no longer room for them, not even at the door. While Jesus was preaching to them, four men came, carrying a man who was paralyzed and could not move. As they could not get near to Jesus on account of the crowd, they tore up the roof over his head. When they had made a hole,they let down the bed on which the man who could not move was lying.

Seeing their faith, Jesus said to him, "Son, your sins are forgiven."
But some of the scribes sitting there said to themselves, "Why should this man say such a thing? He is blaspheming! Who can forgive sins except God alone?"

Knowing at once what they were saying, Jesus said to them, "Why do you say these things to yourselves? Which is easier: to say to the man who cannot move, 'Your sins are forgiven'; or to say, 'Get up, take your bed, and walk'? But that you may know that the Son of Man has the power on earth to forgive sins" (he said to the man who could not walk) "I say to you, Rise, take up your bed, and go to your home." Then the man rose and at once took up his bed and went out in the presence of them all, so that they were all filled with wonder and praised God, saying, "We have never seen anything like this."

JESUS MAKES EVEN WRONG-DOERS HIS FRIENDS

Then Jesus went out again beside the Sea of Galilee; and all the crowd came to him, and he taught them. As he passed along he saw Levi, the son of Alphæus, sitting at the house where taxes were collected, and he said to him, "Come with me." So Levi arose and followed him.

Now while Jesus was eating dinner in Levi's house, many tax-gatherers and sinners sat down with Jesus and his disciples. The scribes and Pharisees, seeing this, said to his disciples, "Does he eat with tax-gatherers and sinners?" On hearing this, Jesus said to them, "Not those who are well, but those who are sick have need of a physician. I did not come to call the righteous but sinners to repentance."

At another time one of the Pharisees invited Jesus to dine with him. SoJesus entered the Pharisee's house and sat down at the table. In the town was a wicked woman who, when she heard that Jesus was sitting at the table in the Pharisee's house, brought an alabaster jar of perfume.

She stood behind at his feet, weeping; and as her tears began to wet his feet, she wiped them with her hair. And she tenderly kissed his feet and poured the perfume over them.

When the Pharisee who had invited him saw it, he said to himself, "If this man were a prophet, he would know about the woman who is touching him, for she is a sinner."

Jesus answered him, "Simon, I have a word to say to you." He replied, "Say it, Master." "There were two men who owed a certain money-lender some silver: one owed him five hundred silver pieces and the other fifty. Neither of them was able to pay anything; so he forgave them both. Now which of them will love him the more?" Simon answered, "I suppose the man who owed the most." Jesus said to him, "You have decided rightly."

Turning to the woman, Jesus said to Simon, "You see this woman? When I came into your house, you gave me no water for my feet; but she has wet my feet with her tears and wiped them with her hair. You gave me no kiss, but she, since I came in, has not ceased tenderly to kiss my feet. You did not pour any oil on my head, but she has poured perfume on my feet. Therefore, I say to you, her sins, though they be many, are forgiven, for she has loved much. He to whom little is forgiven, loves little."

Then Jesus said to her, "Your sins are forgiven." And the other guests began to say to themselves, "Who is this man who even forgives sins?"
But he said to the woman, "Your faith has saved you; go and be at peace."

JESUS FINDS JOY IN ALL HIS WORK

Once when John's disciples and the Pharisees were keeping a fast, people came to Jesus and said, "Why do the disciples of John and the disciples of the Pharisees fast, but your disciples do not fast?"

Jesus said to them, "Can guests fast at a wedding while the bridegroom is with them? As long as they have the bridegroom with them they cannot fast. But the time will come when the bridegroom is taken away from them; then they will fast. No one sews a piece of new cloth on an old coat; otherwise the patch breaks away from it, the new from the old, and the tear is made worse. No man pours new wine into old wine-skins; otherwise the new wine bursts the skins, and both the wine and the wine-skins are lost. Instead new wine is poured into fresh wine-skins."

One Sabbath Jesus was walking through the grain-fields; and his disciples, as they made their way through, began to pull off the heads of the grain. The Pharisees said to him, "Sir, why are they doing things that on the Sabbath are unlawful?"

He said to them, "Have you never read what David did when he and his followers were in need and hungry? how he went into the house of God, when Abiathar was high priest, and ate the holy bread which only the priests are allowed to eat, and gave it also to those who were with him?"

And Jesus said to them, "The Sabbath was made for man, and not man for the Sabbath; so that the Son of Man is master even of the Sabbath."

At another time he went into a synagogue. A man was there whose hand was shrivelled. And they watched Jesus to see whether he would heal him on the Sabbath day, that they might bring a charge against him. Jesus said to the man whose hand was shrivelled, "Rise and come forward."

Then he said to them, "Is it lawful on the Sabbath day to do good or to do harm? To save life or to kill? Who of you, if he has but one sheep and it falls into a hole on the Sabbath, will not take hold of it and lift it out? Is not a man of much greater value than a sheep?"

But they did not answer. Then looking around upon them with sorrow and indignation because they had no sympathy, he said to the man, "Stretch out your hand."

He stretched it out, and his hand was entirely cured. But the Pharisees went out and at once began to plot with the Herodians against him, how they might put him out of the way.

JESUS CALMS THE STORM

Jesus withdrew to the sea with his disciples, and a crowd followed him from Galilee. Also from Judea, Jerusalem, Idumea the other side of the Jordan, and from the country about Tyre and Sidon a great number, having heard what he was doing, came to him. So he told his disciples to have a small boat ready for him to keep him from being crushed by the crowd; for he had healed so many that all who were sick and in trouble were pressing forward to touch him. And whenever those who had evil spirits saw him, they fell down before him and cried, "You are the Son of God." But again and again he commanded them not to tell who he was.

In the evening Jesus said to his disciples, "Let us cross to the other side." So, leaving the crowd, they took him with them in the boat just as he was; and there were other boats with his. A heavy wind-storm arose and the waves began to break into the boat so that it was filling; but Jesus was in the stern asleep on the cushion. So they woke him and said to him, "Master, is it nothing to you that we are lost?" And he awoke and reproved the wind, and said to the sea, "Peace, be still!" And immediately the wind ceased and the sea was calm; and he said to them, "Why are you afraid? Why do you not have faith?" But they were filled with wonder and said to one another, "Who then is he, that even the wind and the sea obey him?"

JESUS HEALS A LITTLE GIRL

When Jesus again crossed the Sea of Galilee in a boat to the other side, a large crowd had gathered to meet him; so he stayed beside the sea. One of the rulers of the synagogue, Jairus by name, came up, and, on seeing Jesus, fell at his feet and earnestly begged him, saying, "My little daughter is dying; come, I beg of you, and place your hands on her that she may be cured and live." So Jesus went with him, and a great crowd followed and pressed about him.

In the crowd was a woman who had suffered from hemorrhage for twelve years and had been treated by many physicians, spending all that she had, yet was none the better, but rather had grown worse. Having heard about Jesus, she came up behind him in the crowd and touched his robe, for she said to herself, "If I can but touch his garments, I shall be cured."

Immediately the hemorrhage stopped, and she knew that she was cured of her disease. Jesus, knowing at once that healing power had gone from him, turned around in the crowd and said, "Who touched my garments?"

His disciples said to him, "You see the crowd pressing around you, and yet do you ask, 'Who touched me?'" But still he looked for her who had done this, until the woman, frightened and trembling, knowing what had happened to her, came forward and fell down before him and told him the truth. He said to her, "Daughter, your faith has cured you. Go and live in peace, and be healed of your disease."

While Jesus was still speaking, messengers came from the house of the ruler of the synagogue, saying, "Your daughter is dead. Why trouble the Master further?" But Jesus, overhearing the message, said to the ruler of the synagogue, "Have no fear, only trust."

Jesus would allow no one to go with him except Peter and James and John the brother of James. When they came to the house of the ruler of the synagogue, he found a crowd of people weeping aloud and wailing.

Entering, Jesus said to them, "Why are you making an uproar and weeping? The child is not dead, but asleep." And they laughed at him scornfully. But he sent them out and took the father and mother of the child and those who were with him into the room where she was.

Then, taking her by the hand, he said to her, "Talitha koumi," which means, "Little girl, arise." To the astonishment of all, the little girl (who was twelve years of age) got up at once and walked about. But Jesus charged them strictly to let no one know of this, and told them to give the little girl something to eat.

JESUS VISITS HIS OLD HOME

Jesus went to Nazareth where he had been brought up. As was his custom, he went into the synagogue on the Sabbath, and stood up to read the lesson. And he was given the scroll of the prophet Isaiah, and on unrolling it he found the place where it is written:

"The Spirit of the Lord is upon me,

For he has called me to preach good news to the poor,

He has sent me to proclaim release to captives,

And recovery of sight to the blind,

To set free those who have been crushed by cruelty,

To proclaim the year when the Lord will show favor."

Then, having rolled up the scroll, he handed it back to the attendant and sat down. The eyes of all in the synagogue were fixed on him, and he said to them, "To-day what is here written is fulfilled in your sight."

As he went on to teach in the synagogue, many who heard him were astonished and said: "Where did he get these teachings? What is this wisdom which has been given him? and what are these wonderful acts of healing that he does? Is he not the carpenter, the son of Mary and the brother of James and Joses and Judas and Simon? Are not his sisters living here among us?" And they would not believe in him. Jesus said to them, "A prophet is not without honor except in his own country and among his relatives and in his own home."

In that place he could do no wonderful acts except laying his hands on a few sick people and healing them; and he was astonished at their lack of faith. So he went about the near-by villages teaching.

JESUS CALLS TOGETHER HIS FRIENDS AND HELPERS

Jesus went up on the hillside near Capernaum and called to him the men whom he wanted, and they came to him. He appointed twelve to be with him and to go out to preach, with power to cast out evil spirits. These were the twelve disciples: Simon to whom he gave also the name Peter, James the son of Zebedee and John his brother, whom he called "Sons of Thunder," Andrew, Philip, Bartholomew, Matthew, Thomas, James the son of Alphæus, Thaddeus, Simon the Zealot, and Judas Iscariot, who at last betrayed him.

Then Jesus went into a house and the crowd gathered again so that it was impossible even to eat a meal. When his relatives heard of this, they set out to get hold of him, for they said, "He is out of his mind."

Standing outside, his mother and his brothers sent word to him to come out to them. He was in the midst of a crowd seated about him when some one said to him, "Here are your mother and your brothers and sisters outside hunting for you." He answered, "Who are my mother and my brothers?"

Then looking around at those who sat in a circle about him, he said, "Here are my mother and my brothers. Whoever does the will of God is my brother and sister and mother."

WHAT JESUS ASKS OF HIS FRIENDS AND HELPERS

Once Jesus entered a certain village where a woman named Martha invited him to her house. She had a sister named Mary who seated herself at Jesus' feet and listened to his words. But Martha was worried by her desire to wait on him, and came and said to him, "Lord, do you not care that my sister has left me to do all the work alone? Tell her to help me." But Jesus said to her, "Martha, Martha, you are anxious and troubled about many things, but few things are necessary, really only one. Mary has chosen the better part, which shall not be taken away from her."

Once when Jesus and his disciples were walking along the road, some one said to him, "I will follow you wherever you go." Jesus said to him, "The foxes have holes and the wild birds their nests, but the Son of Man has no place to lay his head." He said to another, "Follow me"; but the man said, "Let me first go and bury my father." Jesus said to him, "Let the dead bury their dead, but you go and tell about the Kingdom of God."

Still another said, "I will follow you, Lord, but let me first say good-by to my people at home." Jesus said to him, "No one who looks back after having put his hand to the plough is fit for the Kingdom of God."

Once, when crowds were following him, he turned and said to them, "If any one who comes to me is not willing to give up his father and mother and wife and children and brothers and sisters, yes, and his very life, he cannot be my disciple. Whoever does not carry his own cross, as he follows me, cannot be my disciple.

"Who of you, if he wishes to build a tower, does not first sit down and count the cost, to see whether he has money enough to finish it? Otherwise, if he has laid the foundation and is unable to finish the building, all who see it make fun of him and say, 'This man began to build but could not finish!'"

THE WAY TO LEARN FROM JESUS

Jesus taught his disciples, saying, "Do not think that I came to set aside the old law or the teachings of the prophets. I did not come to set them aside but to complete them.

"Come to me, all you who labor and are heavily burdened, and I will give you rest. Take my yoke upon you and learn of me, for I am kind and sympathetic, and you will find rest, for my yoke is easy and my burden light.

"He who hears these words of mine and keeps them in mind will be like a wise man who built his house upon the rock. The rain fell, the floods came, the winds blew and beat upon that house; yet it did not fall, for its foundation was built on the rock.

"He who hears these words of mine but does not keep them in mind will be like a foolish man who built his house upon sand. The rain fell, the floods came, the winds blew and beat upon that house, and it fell, and great was its downfall."

At another time when Jesus was teaching beside the lake, such a large crowd gathered about him that he entered a boat and sat in it, while the crowd stayed on the shore. He then taught them many truths by means of stories, and said, "Listen to me. The sower went out to sow, and as he sowed, some of the seed fell on the road where birds came and ate it up. Some fell on rocky ground, where it had but little soil, and because there was no depth of earth it began to grow at once; but when the sun rose, it was scorched with the heat, and having no root it withered away. Some of the seed fell among thorns, and the thorns grew up and choked it so that it bore nothing. Other seed fell on good soil, and sprouted and grew and bore at the rate of thirty, sixty, and a hundredfold." And he said to them, "Let him who has ears to hear, remember this."

When Jesus was alone, those who were with him and the twelve disciples asked him what this story meant. He said to them, "Do you not see the meaning of this? How then will you understand all my other stories? The sower sows his teaching. The teaching that is sown along the road is like some people who hear but immediately Satan comes and takes away the teaching which has been sown in them.

"And the seed that has been sown on rocky places, is like those people who hear the teaching and receive it at once with joy, but it takes no root in them and they remember it only for a short time.

"The seed sown among thorns is like those who hear the teaching but the pleasures of this life, the desire for wealth and other things makes them forget the teaching, and so it bears no fruit.

"But the seed sown on good soil is like those people who hear the teaching and remember it, and it bears fruit; some thirty, some sixty, and some a hundredfold.

"Can a blind man guide a blind man? Will not both fall into a ditch? A disciple is not above his teacher; but every pupil when perfectly trained will be like his teacher.

"No good tree bears rotten fruit; neither does a rotten tree bear good fruit; for each tree is known by its own fruit. Figs are not gathered from thorns, nor grapes picked from a bramble-bush. From the good stored in his heart the good man brings forth goodness, but the evil man from his evil store brings forth evil; for the mouth speaks that with which the heart is filled.

"You are the light of the world. A city on a hill cannot be hidden. One does not light a candle to put it under a basket but on a stand, where it shall give light to all who are in the house. So let your light shine before men that they may see your good deeds and praise your heavenly Father."

THE REWARDS FOR FOLLOWING JESUS' TEACHINGS

James and John, the sons of Zebedee, once came to Jesus and said, "Master, we want you to do for us what we shall ask." So he said, "What do you want me to do for you?" They answered, "When you enter into your kingly glory, let one of us sit on your right hand and one on your left." But Jesus said to them, "You do not know what you are asking. Can you drink the cup of woe that I am to drink, or be baptized with the baptism of suffering with which I am to be baptized?"

They said to him, "We can."

Jesus said, "You will drink the cup that I am to drink and be baptized with my baptism, but to sit on my right hand and on my left is not mine to give; for it is for those for whom it has been prepared."

When the ten other disciples heard this request, they were at first angry with James and John, but Jesus called them to him and said, "You know that those who are rulers in foreign countries lord it over those under them, and their great men have authority over them; but it is not so among you. Whoever wishes to be great among you must serve you, and whoever wishes to be first among you must be ready to be the servant of all. For I did not come to be served but to be of service to others, and to give my life so as to secure freedom for many."

Then he took a little child and set him in their midst. And taking him in his arms, he said to them, "Whoever receives a little child like this, in my name, receives me; and whoever receives me receives not only me, but God who sent me. Whoever gives one of these little ones even a cup of cold water to drink because he is my disciple will, I tell you, not lose his reward.

"When the Son of Man comes in his glory and with him all the angels, he will sit upon his glorious throne, and all people shall be gathered before him. And he will separate them one from another as a shepherd separates the sheep from the goats, placing the sheep on his right hand and the goats on his left.

"Then the King will say to those on his right, 'Come, you whom my Father has blessed, enter into possession of the kingdom prepared for you since the creation of the world; for I was hungry and you gave me food, I was thirsty and you gave me drink, I was a stranger and you welcomed me, I was naked and you clothed me, I was sick and you cared for me, I was in prison and you came to me.'

"Then the upright will answer him, 'Lord, when did we see you hungry and feed you? Or thirsty and give you drink? When did we see you a stranger and welcome you? Or naked and clothe you? Or when did we see you sick or in prison and come to you?' The King will answer them, 'Truly, I say to you, as you have done it even to the least of these my brothers, you have done it to me.'"

GOD'S LOVE EVEN FOR SINNERS

Because tax-gathers and sinners kept coming to Jesus to hear him, the Pharisees and scribes complained, "This man welcomes sinners and even eats with them!" So he told them this story: "What man of you, if he has a hundred sheep and loses one, does not leave the ninety-nine in the wilderness and go and hunt for the lost sheep until he finds it? And when he has found it, he joyfully puts it on his shoulders and when he gets home calls together his friends and says, 'Rejoice with me, for I have found the sheep that I lost.' So, I tell you, there will be more joy in heaven over one sinner who is truly sorry and promises to do right than over ninety-nine upright men who have no need to do so.

"Or which one of you women, if she has ten silver coins but has lost one, does not light a lamp, sweep the house thoroughly, and search carefully until she finds it? After finding it she calls together her friends and neighbors and says, 'Rejoice with me, for I have found the coin that I lost.' So, I tell you, there is rejoicing among the angelsof God over one sinner who is truly sorry and promises to do right."

Jesus said, "There was a man who had two sons. The younger said to his father, 'Father, give me the part of your property that belongs to me.' So the Father divided his property between his two sons. A few days later, the younger son got together all that he had and went into a distant country where he wasted his money in reckless living. After he had spent it all, there was a great famine in the land, and he began to be in want. So he agreed to work for a man of that country, who sent him into his fields to feed swine; and he was ready to eat even the pods that the swine were eating, for no one gave him food. But when he came to himself he said,

'How many of my father's hired servants have more than enough to eat while I die here of hunger! I will go to my father and say, 'Father, I have sinned against God and against you. I am no longer worthy to be called your son. Treat me as one of your hired servants.'

"So he went to his father. But while he was still a long way off, his father saw him and felt pity for him, and ran and threw his arms about his neck and tenderly kissed him. Then his son said to him, 'Father, I have sinned against God and against you. I am no longer worthy to be called your son.' But the father said to his servants, 'Quick, bring a coat, the best, and put it on him and put a ring on his finger and sandals on his feet. And bring the fatted calf, kill it, and let us eat and be merry; for this son of mine was dead but has come back to life, he was lost but has been found.' So they began to make merry.

"Now the elder son was out in the fields, and as he came near the house he heard music and dancing. And he called one of the servants and asked what all this meant. The servant said to him, 'Your brother has come, and your father has killed the fatted calf because he has him back safe and sound.' And he was angry and would not go in so his father came out to reason with him, but he answered, 'See all these many years I have worked for you and never disobeyed one of your ommands, yet you never gave me so much as a young goat that I might have a feast with my friends. But now when this son of yours comes, who has wasted your money with wicked women, you kill the fatted calf for him!' His father answered, 'Son, you are with me always and all that I have is yours; but it was right to make merry and rejoice because of your brother, for he was dead but has come back to life, he was lost but has been found.'"

GOD'S READINESS TO ANSWER PRAYER

Jesus said: "Ask and you will receive, seek and you will find, knock and the door will be opened to you; for every one who asks receives, and he who seeks finds, and to him who knocks the door will be opened.

"What man is there among you, who if his son asks him for a loaf of bread, will give him a stone? Or if he asks for a fish, will give him a snake? Then if you, evil as you are, know how to give good gifts to your children, how much more will your Father in heaven give good things to those who ask him.

"Also I tell you: if two of you on earth agree about that for which you ask, it will be granted to you by my Father in heaven. For where two or three have gathered together in my name, I am there with them."

HOW TO PRAY

The apostles said to Jesus, "Help us to have greater faith." But he said, "If you had faith even the size of a mustard-seed and said to this mulberry-tree, 'Be rooted up and be planted in the sea,' it would obey you."

Again he said to them, "Have faith in God. Indeed I tell you that if any one will say to this hill, 'Throw yourself into the sea,' and has no doubt in his heart but believes that what he says will come to pass, it shall be done for him. Therefore, I say to you, believe that whatever you ask for in prayer you have received, and it shall be yours. And whenever you stand up to pray, if any one has done wrong to you, forgive him, that your Father in heaven may also forgive you your wrong-doing."

When Jesus was praying at a certain place and had finished, one of his disciples said to him, "Lord, teach us to pray as John taught his disciples."

So he said to them, "When you pray, say: 'Our Father who art in heaven, hallowed be thy name, thy kingdom come, thy will be done on earth as it is in heaven. Give us this day our daily bread, and forgive us our wrong-doings as we have forgiven those who have wronged us. Help us to resist temptation and deliver us from evil.'

"When you pray, do not do as the hypocrites who like to stand and pray in the synagogues and on the corners of the main streets so as to be seen by men. I tell you, they have received their full reward! But when you pray, go into your room, close the door, and pray to your Father who is found in secret, and your Father who sees what is done in secret will give you your reward.

"When you pray do not say the same things over and over as do the heathen, who believe that they will be heard because of their many words. Do not do as they do. Your Father knows what things you need before you ask him."

WHY WE SHOULD TRUST GOD

"Do not be anxious about your life, what you shall eat, or what you shall wear. Does not life mean more than food, and the body more than clothing? Consider how the birds of the air neither sow nor reap nor gather into barns, and yet your heavenly Father feeds them. Are you not worth far more than they? Are not two sparrows sold for a penny? Yet not one of them falls to the ground without your Father's knowledge. As for you, the very hairs of your head are numbered. Then have no fear, for you are worth far more than the sparrows.

"Which of you by being anxious can add a single foot to his height? And why be anxious about what you wear? Consider the lilies of the field, how they grow! They neither toil nor spin, and yet I tell you, not even Solomon in all his splendor was clothed like one of these. Now if God so clothes the grass of the field which is alive to-day but to-morrow is thrown into the oven, is it not far more certain that he will clothe you, O men of little faith?

"Do not be anxious then and say, 'What shall we eat or what shall we drink or with what shall we be clothed?' For all these things the heathen are seeking, but your heavenly Father knows that you need all these things. Seek first to do right as he would have you do, and all these other things will be given to you. Therefore, do not be anxious about to-morrow, for to-morrow will take care of itself."

THE KINGDOM OF GOD

Once when little children were brought to Jesus that he might touch them, the disciples found fault with those who brought them. When Jesus saw it, he was displeased and said to his disciples, "Allow the little children to come to me; and do not forbid them, for of such as these is the Kingdom of God. I tell you, whoever will not accept the Kingdom of God like a little child, will never enter it." Then he took the children in his arms, laid his hands on them, and lovingly blessed them.

One Sabbath day Jesus went to dine at the house of a leading Pharisee. One of the guests said to him, "Fortunate is he who will have a share in the Kingdom of God."

But Jesus said to him, "A man once gave a great dinner and invited many guests. At dinner-time he sent out his servant to say to those who had been invited, 'Come, for everything is now ready.' But all of them began to make excuses. The first said, 'I have bought a field and must go and look at it. I must ask you to excuse me.' Another said, 'I have bought five yoke of oxen and am on my way to try them. I must ask you to excuseme.' Another said, 'I have just married and so I cannot come.'

"The servant returned and reported these answers to his master. Then the master of the house was angry and said to his servant, 'Go out at once into the streets and alleys of the city, and bring in the poor, the crippled, the blind, and the lame.' When the servant reported, 'Sir, your order has been carried out, yet there is still room,' the master said to him, 'Go out into the highways and the country lanes and compel people to come, so that my house may be filled; for I tell you, that not one of those who were first invited shall taste of my dinner.'"

Once when Jesus was walking along the road, a man ran up and knelt before him and asked, "Good Master, what must I do that I may be sure of eternal life?" Jesus said to him, "Why do you call me good? No one is good except one only: God. You know the commandments: 'Do not commit adultery. Do not murder. Do not steal. Do not bear false witness. Do not be dishonest. Honor your father and mother.'"

He said to him, "Master, I have kept all these commands from my youth." Looking upon him, Jesus loved him and said, "One thing you lack; go, sell all that you have and give to the poor, and you will have treasure in heaven. Then come with me." But when the man heard this, he looked sad, and he went away in sorrow, for he had great wealth.

Then Jesus looked around and said to his disciples, "How hard it is for those who have wealth to enter the Kingdom of God!" They were surprised at his words, but again he said, "Children, how hard it is for those who trust in wealth to enter the Kingdom of God. It is easier for a camel to go through a needle's eye than for a rich man to enter the Kingdom of God."

And they were so astonished that they said, "Then who can be saved?" Jesus looked at them and said, "With men it is impossible, but not with God, for with God everything is possible."

THE TWO GREAT COMMANDMENTS

Once a lawyer asked Jesus, "What is the most important of all the commandments?" Jesus answered, "The most important is: 'The Lord our God is one Lord; and you shall love the Lord your God with your whole heart, with your whole soul, with your whole mind and with your whole strength.'

"The second is this: 'You shall love your neighbor as yourself.' There is no other commandment greater than these."

The lawyer said to him, "Teacher, you have rightly and truly said, 'There is one God and there is none other. Also to love him, with all one's heart, and with all one's understanding, and with all one's strength, and to love one's neighbor as one loves himself is far more than all whole-burnt offerings and sacrifices.'"

When Jesus saw that the lawyer had answered wisely, he said to him, "You are not far from the Kingdom of God."

THE REWARDS OF MODESTY AND UNSELFISHNESS

Once Jesus went into the house of a leading Pharisee to dine. When he saw how the guests chose the best places, he gave them this advice: "When any one invites you to a marriage feast, do not sit down in the best place, for perhaps the host has invited some one of higher rank than yourself. Then the host will come to you and say, 'Make room for this man,' and with shame you will take the lowest place.

"Instead, when you are invited, go and sit down in the lowest place, so that when your host comes he may say to you, 'Friend, come up higher.' Then you will be honored in the sight of all your fellow guests. For every one who puts himself forward will be humbled, but he who does not put himself forward will be honored."

Then Jesus said to his host, "When you give a dinner or a supper, do not invite your friends or brothers or relatives or rich neighbors, for they will invite you in return and you be repaid. But when you give a feast, invite the poor, the crippled, the lame and the blind. Then you will be blessed. For they have no way of repaying you, and you will be rewarded when the upright rise from the dead."

Peter said to him, "But we have left everything and have followed you."
Jesus answered, "I tell you, there is no one who has left home or brothers or sisters or mother or father or children or lands for my sake and for the good cause, who does not receive a hundredfold as much at this present time: houses, brothers, sisters, mothers, children, and lands, along with persecution, and in the time to come eternal life. Butmany who are first now will be last, and the last will be first."

HOW TO USE MONEY

A man from the crowd once said to Jesus, "Master, tell my brother to give me my share of the property that belongs to us." Jesus answered, "Man, who made me your judge to divide between you?" Then to the people he said, "Take care that you do not become greedy for wealth, for life does not consist in having more things than you need."

And he told them this story: "The land of a certain rich man bore large crops; so he thought to himself, 'What am I to do, for I have no place to store my crops.' Then he said, 'This is what I will do: I will pull down my barns and build larger ones in which I can store all my grain and goods. Then I will say to myself, Now you have plenty of things laid up for many years to come; take your ease, eat, drink and be happy.'

"But God said to him, 'Foolish man! This very night your life is required of you, and who will have all the things that you have gathered?' So it is with the man who lays up wealth for himself instead of that which in the sight of God is the true wealth.

"Do not store up for yourselves treasures on earth where moth and rust destroy, and where thieves break in and steal; but store up for yourselves treasures in heaven where neither moth nor rust destroys, and where thieves do not break in and steal. For where your treasure is, there will your heart be also.

"No man can serve two masters: either he will hate one and love the other, or else he will be loyal to one and untrue to the other. You cannot worship both God and wealth."

Once as Jesus was sitting opposite the treasury of the Temple, he watched the way in which the people put in their money. Many rich men were putting in large sums, but a poor woman came and dropped in two small coins worth less than a penny. He called his disciples and said to them, "I tell you, this poor widow has given more than all the rest who have put their money into the treasury, for they have given out of their plenty, but she out of her poverty has given all that she has, even that which is needed to keep her alive."

DIFFERENT WAYS OF USING TALENTS

"The Kingdom of Heaven is like a man who before going abroad called his servants and gave what he had into their charge. To one he gave five talents, to another two, and to another one, each according to what he was able to do. Then the man went on his journey.

"The servant who had received five talents went at once and traded with them and gained five more talents. In the same way the one who had received two gained two more. But he who had received one talent went away and dug a hole in the ground and hid his master's money.

"After a long time the master of those servants came back and settled his accounts with them. When the one who had received five talents came bringing five more, he said, 'Master, you gave me five talents. See, I have gained five more.' His master said to him 'Well done, good and faithful servant! You have been faithful over a few things, I will put you in charge of many things. Share your master's happiness.'

"The one who had received the two talents also came and said, 'Master, you gave me two talents. See, I have gained two more.' His master said to him, 'Well done, good and faithful servant! You have been faithful over a few things, I will put you in charge of many things. Share your master's happiness.'

"Then he who had received one talent came and said, 'Master, I knew that you are a hard man, reaping where you have not sown and gathering where you have not winnowed; so I was afraid and hid your talent in the ground. There you have what belongs to you.'

"But his master answered, 'Idle, worthless servant! You knew that I reap where I have not sown and gather where I have not winnowed. You ought therefore to have put my money in the hands of bankers and on my return I would have received it with interest. Take my talent away from him and give it to the servant who has the ten talents; for to every one who has shall more be given and he shall have plenty; but from him who has only a little, even what he has shall be taken away. Throw this worthless servant into the outer darkness where men shall wail and grind their teeth.'"

THE GOOD SAMARITAN

Once a lawyer stood up to test Jesus with this question, "Master, what shall I do to receive eternal life?" Jesus said to him, "What is written in the law? How does it read?" He answered, "You shall love the Lord your God with all your heart, with all your soul, and with all your strength and with all your mind; also your neighbor as yourself." Jesus said to him, "You have answered correctly; do this and you will live."

But wishing to justify himself he said to Jesus, "Who is my neighbor?"

Jesus answered, "A certain man going down from Jerusalem to Jericho fell in with robbers who after stripping and beating him went away, leaving him half dead. Now it happened that a certain priest was going by the same road, but when he saw the man, he passed by on the other side.

"In the same way a Levite, when he came to the place, looked at the man and passed by on the other side. But a Samaritan, travelling along, came near to where the man was, and when he saw him he was filled with pity. He came to him and bound up his wounds, pouring on them oil and wine. Then he set him on his own beast, brought him to an inn, and took care of him. The next day he took out two pieces of money and gave them to the inn-keeper, saying, 'Take care of him, and whatever more you spend I will pay you when I return.'

"Which of these three do you think proved neighbor to the man who fell in with robbers?" He said, "The man who took pity on him." Jesus said to him, "Then go and do likewise."

THE WAY TO TREAT THOSE WHO WRONG US

"If your brother wrongs you, go, show him his fault when you and he are alone. If he listens to you, you have won over your brother. Even though he wrongs you seven times in a day, if he turns to you seven times and says, 'I am sorry,' you shall forgive him."

Peter came and said to Jesus, "Master, how often am I to let my brother wrong me and forgive him? Seven times?"

Jesus said to him, "I tell you, not seven times but seventy times seven.

"That is why the Kingdom of Heaven may be compared to a king who wished to settle his accounts with his servants. When he had begun to settle them, a man was brought to him who owed him ten thousand talents; but as he was unable to pay, the master ordered that he be sold, together with his wife and children and all that he had, in payment of the debt.

At this the servant threw himself on the ground and begged of him, 'Master, have patience with me and I will pay you all I owe you.' Then the master out of pity for him let him go and forgave him his debt.

"But as soon as the servant went out, he found one of his fellow servants who owed him one-sixtieth of a talent, and he seized him by the throat and said, 'Pay me what you owe me.' The man fell down and begged him, 'Have patience with me and I will pay you.' But he would not and had him imprisoned until he should pay what was due.

"Now when his fellow servants saw what had been done, they were troubled and came and told their master what had happened. Then the master called him and said, 'You wicked servant! When you begged of me, I forgave you all your debt. Should you not then show the same mercy to your fellow that I showed to you?' And in anger his master turned him over to the jailers until he should pay all that was due. So also will my heavenly Father do to you unless each of you sincerely forgives his brother."

THE GOLDEN RULE

"You have heard the saying, 'You shall love your neighbor and hate your enemy.' But I say to you, love your enemies, bless those who curse you, do good to those who hate you, and pray for those who persecute you, that you may become sons of your Father in heaven; for he makes his sun to rise on the wicked and the good alike, and sends rain on both those who do right and those who do wrong. For if you love only those who love you, what reward have you earned? Do not even the tax-gatherers as much? And if you show courtesy only to your friends, what more are you doing than others? Do not even the heathen do as much? You must therefore become perfect, even as your heavenly Father is perfect.

"Therefore, whatever you wish that men should do to you, do even so to them."

THE PEOPLE WHO ARE REALLY HAPPY

Jesus said to his disciples:

"Blessed are the poor in spirit,

For theirs is the Kingdom of Heaven.

Blessed are the meek,

For they shall inherit the earth.

Blessed are they who mourn,

For they shall be comforted.

Blessed are they who hunger and thirst for righteousness,

For they shall be satisfied.

Blessed are the merciful,

For they shall receive mercy.

Blessed are the pure in heart,

For they shall see God.

Blessed are the peacemakers,

For they shall be called the sons of God.

Blessed are they who are persecuted because of their righteousness,

For theirs is the Kingdom of Heaven.

Blessed are you when you are reviled, persecuted, and falsely maligned

because of loyalty to me;

Rejoice and be glad, for great is your reward in heaven, for so the

prophets were persecuted who came before you."

JESUS SENDS OUT THE FIRST MISSIONARIES

Jesus went through all the towns and villages, teaching in their synagogues, preaching the good news about the Kingdom of God, and healing all kinds of diseases and weaknesses. At sight of the crowds, troubled and scattered like sheep without a shepherd, he was filled with pity, and said to his disciples, "This is a large harvest, but the laborers are few. Pray to the lord of the harvest to send laborers into his fields."

Then calling the twelve disciples, he sent them out two by two; and he gave them power over evil spirits. He told them to take nothing for their journey but a staff.

Also he said, "Go your way. Remember that I send you out as lambs among wolves. Take with you neither purse nor bag nor an extra pair of shoes, and do not stop to greet any one on the road. Whatever household you first enter, say, 'Peace to this house!'

And if the man living there is worthy, your peace will rest upon him; but if not, it shall return to you. Stay at the same house, eating and drinking what they give you, for the laborer deserves his wages. Do not go from one house to another.

"Also in whatever town you enter, if the people receive you, eat what they set before you. Heal those in that town who are ill, and tell them, 'The Kingdom of God is near you.' But if you enter any town where the people do not receive you, go out into its streets and say, 'Even the dust of your town which clings to our feet, we wipe off in protest against you.' But know this: that the Kingdom of God is at hand. I tell you, on that day it will be better for Sodom than for that city.

"Do not give to the dogs that which is sacred, nor throw your pearls before swine, for fear that they trample them under their feet and then turn back to attack you. He who hears you, hears me; he who rejects you, rejects me; he who rejects me, rejects him who sent me."

So Jesus' disciples went out and preached so as to lead men to be sorry for their sins and live as they should. They also cast out many evil spirits and cured many sick by pouring oil upon them. Then returning to Jesus they told him what they had done and taught.

JESUS PRAISES JOHN THE BAPTIST

When John heard in prison what Jesus was doing, he sent his disciples to ask him, "Are you the Promised One who is coming, or are we to look for some one else?" Jesus answered them, "Go and tell John what you see and hear: the blind see, the lame walk, the lepers are made clean, the deaf hear, the dead are brought back to life, and the poor have the good news told to them. Blessed is the man who does not lose faith in me."

As the disciples of John went away, Jesus talked to the people about John: "What did you go into the wilderness to see? A reed shaken by the wind? Then what did you go out to see? A man wearing fine clothes? Men dressed like that live in palaces. But why did you go out? To see a prophet? Yes, I tell you, and more than a prophet! This is he of whom it is written:

"'Behold, I send my messenger before you,
Who shall make the way ready for you.'

"I tell you, no man has appeared who is greater than John the Baptist; and yet he who is least in the Kingdom of God is greater than he.

"To what shall I compare the people of to-day? They are like children sitting in the market-places, who call to their playmates and say:

"'We played the pipes for you but you would not dance;

We cried but you would not lament.'

For John came neither eating nor drinking, and men said, 'He has an evil spirit!' The Son of Man came eating and drinking, and men say, 'He is a great eater and drinker, a friend of tax-gatherers and sinners!' But what I do shows that I am wise and right."

Now when Herod's birthday came, the daughter of Herodias danced in public and delighted him. Thereupon he promised with an oath that he would give her whatever she might ask. Prompted by her mother, she said to him, "Give me here on a dish the head of John the Baptist."

Although the king did not wish to do it, yet because of his oath and his guests he ordered that it be given her. So he commanded that John be beheaded in prison, and his head was brought on a dish and given to the girl, and she brought it to her mother. Then John's disciples came and carried away the body to bury it.

JESUS FEEDS THE HUNGRY

When Herod the ruler of Galilee heard what Jesus was doing, he was greatly puzzled, for some said that John had come back from the dead, some that Elijah had appeared, and others that one of the old prophets had come to life again. Herod said, "I have beheaded John; but who is this of whom I hear these stories?" And he tried to find him.

Then Jesus said to his disciples, "Come by yourselves to some quiet place and rest a while"; for so many people were coming and going that the disciples could not find time even to eat. So they went in a boat by themselves to a quiet place; but many people saw and knew them as they went, and, running from all the towns, they arrived before them. When Jesus landed he found a large crowd waiting for him. Feeling sorry for them because they were like sheep without a shepherd, he began to teach them many things.

As it was already late in the day, his disciples came to him and said, "This place is far away from any town and it is now late. Send the people away to the neighboring farms and villages to buy food for themselves." But he answered "Give them some food." They replied, "Are we to go and buy two hundred silver pieces' worth of food for them?" He said, "Go and see how many loaves you have." When they found out, they said, "Five, and two fishes." Then he commanded them to make the people sit down in groups on the green grass.

So they sat down in companies of a hundred and of fifty. Then Jesus took the five loaves and the two fishes, and, looking up to heaven, he blessed the loaves, and broke them in pieces; and he gave to the disciples to set before the people. He also divided the two fishes among them, and all ate and had enough. Then they picked up twelve baskets full of broken pieces of the bread and fish, although the number of the people who had shared them was five thousand.

Then Jesus had his disciples enter the boat and cross before him to Bethsaida, while he himself sent away the crowd. After sending them away, he climbed a hill to pray. When evening came the boat was in the middle of the sea and he alone on the land. Seeing that they were having trouble as they rowed, for the wind was against them, he went to them at about three o'clock in the early morning, walking on the sea as if he intended to pass them. When they saw him walking on the sea, they believed that he was a ghost and cried out, for all saw him and were frightened; but he spoke to them at once, saying, "Have courage, it is I; do not be afraid." Then he went on board the boat and the wind dropped, but they were greatly astonished for they had not learned the lesson of the loaves, for they were slow to understand its meaning.

After crossing the sea they landed at Gennesaret and fastened the boat. As soon as they had gone ashore, the people knew Jesus and searched all that part of the country, and whenever they heard that he had come to a certain place, they brought to him the sick on their beds. In every city or town or village to which he went people would lay their sick in the market-place and beg him to let them touch even the edge of his robe. And all who touched him were made well.

JESUS TELLS WHAT IT MEANS TO BE CLEAN

The Pharisees and some of the scribes who had come from Jerusalem went together to Jesus, because they had seen that some of his disciples ate their food without washing their hands as the scribes thought necessary.

For the Pharisees and all the Jews always wash their hands up to the wrists before eating. So the Pharisees and scribes asked him, "Why do not your disciples obey the old custom instead of eating food with unwashed hands?" Jesus said to them, "Well did Isaiah prophesy about you hypocrites: 'This people honors me with their lips, but their heart is not with me; their worship is worthless, for they teach what are only commands of men.' You set aside the command of God and follow that of men.

"Moses said, 'Honor your father and your mother,' and, 'He who speaks evil of father or mother shall die.' But you say, 'If a man says to his father or to his mother, What you were to have received from me is given to God,' you hold that he need not do anything for his father or mother. In this way you set aside the command of God in favor of the teaching which you have handed down; and you do many other things like that."

Then calling the crowd to him again, he said to them, "Hear me, all of you, and understand. Nothing can make a man unclean by going into him from outside. It is what comes from him that makes him unclean, for from within, from the heart of man, come evil thoughts, acts of theft, murder, greed, wickedness, deceit, impure thoughts, envy, slander, pride, and recklessness. All these evil things come from within, and they make a man unclean."

JESUS IS KIND TO A STRANGER

Certain Pharisees came to Jesus and said to him, "Go away from here; for Herod wishes to kill you." He said to them, "Go and tell that fox, 'See, I cast out evil spirits and cure the sick to-day and to-morrow, but on the third day I must go on my way; for it cannot be that a prophet will be put to death anywhere except in Jerusalem.'"

Jesus left Capernaum and went into the land of Tyre and Sidon. Going into a house, he wished that no one should know that he was there, but he could not escape notice. Soon a woman whose little daughter had an evil spirit heard of him and came and knelt at his feet. Now the woman was a heathen of the Phœnician race. She begged him to drive the evil spirit out of her daughter, but he said to her, "Let the children of Israel first be fed, for it is not fair to take their bread and throw it to the dogs!"

She answered him, "True, sir, yet the little dogs under the table do eat the children's crumbs." He said to her, "Because of this answer go to your home; the evil spirit has gone out of your daughter." On returning home she found the child lying on the bed and the evil spirit gone from her.

Jesus again left the land of Tyre and passed through Sidon to the Sea of Galilee, crossing the land of Decapolis. The people brought to him a deaf man, who also stammered; and they begged Jesus to lay his hand on him.

Jesus took the man away from the crowd, put his fingers into the man's ears, touched his tongue with saliva, and looking up to heaven, sighed, and said to him,

"Ephphatha" (which means "Open"). And at once, the man could hear and could talk without stammering.

Then Jesus told them to tell no one, but in spite of what he said the people kept telling about it, saying: "How well he has done everything! He even makes the deaf hear, and the dumb speak."

JESUS MAKES AN HEROIC CHOICE

On their way to the villages of Cæsarea Philippi Jesus asked his disciples, "Who do people say I am?" They told him, "John the Baptist; others say, 'Elijah'; some say, 'One of the prophets.'" Then he said to them, "But you yourselves, who do you say that I am?" Peter answered him, "You are the Christ." But he strictly charged them to tell no one that he was the Christ.

Then Jesus began to explain to his disciples that he must suffer many things and be rejected by the elders and high priests and scribes and be killed, but that after three days he would rise from the dead. This he said openly; and Peter tried to reprove him. But Jesus turned and, looking upon his disciples, reproved Peter, saying, "Away with you, Satan, for your mind is not on the things of God but of men."

Then Jesus called the crowd and his disciples to him, and said to them, "If any one wishes to follow me, let him forget himself, take up his cross, and come with me. For any one who is thinking only of saving his life, will lose it; but whoever loses his life for my sake and for the sake of the good news, will save it. What does it profit a man to gain the whole world and lose his soul? For what could a man give in exchange for his soul? Whoever is ashamed of me and my teachings in this sinful world, of him I will be ashamed when I come in the glory of my Father with the holy angels."

JESUS IS GLORIFIED

Six days later Jesus took Peter, James and John up a high mountain where they were alone, and in their presence he was transfigured. His clothes glistened with a dazzling whiteness such as no bleaching could give on earth. And there appeared to them Elijah and Moses, who talked with Jesus.

Then Peter said, "Master, it is fortunate that we are here. Let us make three tabernacles, one for you, one for Moses, and one for Elijah." (For in his terror he did not know what to say.) Then a cloud came and overshadowed them, and a voice from the cloud said, "This is my Beloved Son; give heed to him." And suddenly, looking around, they saw no one with them but Jesus.

As they came down from the mountain, he commanded them to tell no one what they had seen until after he had risen from the dead. And they obeyed the command but discussed among themselves what "rising from the dead" meant.

Therefore they asked him, "How is it that the scribes say, 'Elijah must first come'?" He answered, "Elijah is to come first to restore everything. And what is written about the Son of Man? Is it not that he is to endure great suffering and be despised? But I tell you, Elijah has come, and they have done to him what they pleased, even as it is written of him."

JESUS TELLS HOW ONE MAY BECOME GREAT

Leaving Cæsarea Philippi, Jesus and his disciples passed through Galilee; but he wished no one to know of this, for he was teaching his disciples. He said to them, "The Son of Man will be betrayed and men will put him to death, but in three days he will rise from the dead." But they did not understand his meaning and were afraid to ask.

When they had reached Capernaum and were in the house, he asked them, "What were you arguing about on the way?" But they made no reply, for they had been disputing on the way about which of them was greatest. Sitting down, he called the twelve disciples, and said, "If any one wishes to be first, he will be last of all and servant of all."

Then he took a little child and set him by his side and with his arm around him said to them, "Whoever receives a little child like this in my name, receives me, and whoever receives me, receives not only me, but God whosent me."

JESUS MAKES THE WICKED ZACCHEUS HIS FRIEND

As Jesus passed through Jericho a man named Zaccheus, who was the chief tax-gatherer and rich, tried to see what Jesus was like, but could not on account of the crowd and because he was short. So he ran ahead and climbed into a sycamore-tree to see Jesus, for he was to pass that way. When Jesus came to the place, he looked up and said to him, "Zaccheus, come down, for to-day I must stay at your house." And Zaccheus came down quickly and welcomed him joyfully.

Then all who saw this began to find fault, saying, "He has gone to eat with a man who is a sinner." But Zaccheus stood up and said to Jesus, "Lord, I will give half of all that I have to the poor; and to every man whom I have cheated out of anything I will give back four times as much."

And Jesus said to him, "To-day salvation has come to this house, for you have proved yourself to be a true son of Abraham. For the Son of Man came to seek and to save the lost."

JESUS IS GLADLY WELCOMED BY THE PEOPLE

As Jesus was leaving Jericho with his disciples, followed by a large crowd, there sat by the road a blind beggar, Bartimæus (the son of Timæus). When he heard that it was Jesus of Nazareth, he cried out, "Jesus, son of David, have pity on me!" Many reproved him, saying, "Keep still," but he cried out the more, "Son of David, have pity on me!"

Jesus stopped and said, "Call him." So they called the blind man and said, "Have courage! Get up, he has sent for you." Throwing off his cloak, he sprang up and came to Jesus. Jesus said to him, "What do you want me to do for you?" The blind man answered, "Master, let me receive my sight." Then Jesus said to him, "Go your way, your faith has healed you." And at once he received his sight, and followed Jesus along the road.

When Jesus and those with him were drawing near to Jerusalem and had reached Bethpage and Bethany, near the Mount of Olives, he sent two of his disciples ahead, saying, "Go into the village over there. As soon as you enter it, you will find a colt tied, which no one has ever ridden. Untie it and bring it here. If any one asks you, 'Why are you doing that?' say, 'The Master needs it and will immediately send it back.'"

So they left him and found a colt tied, outside a door, on the street. As they untied it, some of the men standing there said, "What are you doing, untying the colt?" The disciples answered as Jesus had told them, and the men let them take it. When they had brought it to Jesus, they threw their cloaks upon it, and he mounted it.

Many also spread their clothes on the road, while others strewed leafy branches cut from the fields; and people in front and behind kept shouting:

"God save him!
Blessed is he who comes in the name of the Lord!
Blessed is the coming Kingdom of our father David!
God on high, save him!"

Jesus entered Jerusalem and went into the Temple. And when he had looked about, because it was already late in the day, he went out to Bethany with his twelve disciples.

JESUS FIGHTS WRONG IN THE TEMPLE

About this time certain people came to tell Jesus of the Galileans whom Pilate had killed while they were offering sacrifices. He said to them, "Do you believe that these Galileans were worse sinners than the rest? No, I tell you; and unless you are sorry for your sins and do right, you too will all likewise perish. Or those eighteen men who were killed by the fall of the tower of Siloam--do you suppose that they were worse sinners than the rest of the people of Jerusalem? No, I tell you; and unless you are sorry for your sins and do right, you too will all perish."

Then Jesus went into the Temple, and drove out those who were buying and selling there. He upset the tables of the money-changers, and the seats of those who sold doves, and would allow no one to carry any goods through the Temple. For he said to them, "Is it not written, 'My house shall be called a house of prayer for all nations'? But you have made it a den of robbers!" When the chief priests and scribes heard of it, they began to look for some way of putting him to death, for they feared him because all the people were deeply stirred by his teachings. But each evening he and his disciples left the city.

Then once more Jesus and his disciples entered Jerusalem, and as he was walking about the Temple, some high priests and scribes and elders came and asked him, "By what right are you doing these things, and who gave you this right?" Jesus answered, "I will ask you a question; answer me, and I will tell you by what right I do such things. What about John's baptism? Was it from God or from men? Answer me." They argued among themselves, saying, "If we answer, 'From God,' he will ask, 'Why then did you not believe in him?' But if we say, 'From men'"--

they were afraid of the people, for the people believed that John was truly a prophet. So they answered Jesus, "We do not know." He said to them,"Then I will not tell you by what right I do these things.

"But give me your opinion. A man who had two sons went to one of them and said, 'Son, go and work in the vineyard to-day.' And the young man answered, 'I will not'; but afterward changed his mind and went. Then the man went with the same request to the other son, who said, 'I will go, sir'; but he did not go. Which of the two did as his father wished?"

They answered, "The first." Jesus said to them, "I tell you that tax-gatherers and sinners will enter the Kingdom of God before you; for John showed you the way to an upright life, and you did not believe him. But the tax-gatherers and sinners believed him; and even when you saw, you would not say that you were wrong and believe in him.

"Listen to this: There was a landowner who planted a vineyard, and set a hedge around it, dug a pit for the wine-press, and built a watch-tower. Then he leased it to tenants and went to another country.

At vintage time he sent his servants to the tenants to collect the fruits of the vineyard, but they took the servants and flogged one, stoned another, and killed another. Then he sent other servants, more than at first, but they did the same to these. Finally he sent his son, saying to himself, 'They will respect my son.' But the tenants said to one another, 'This is the heir. Come, let us kill him and get his inheritance.' So they threw him out of the vineyard and killed him. Now, when the owner of the vineyard comes, what will he do to these tenants?"

They said, "He will destroy the wretches and lease the vineyard toothers who will give him the fruits in their season."

Jesus said to them, "Have you never read in the scriptures:

"'The stone which the builders rejected
Has been made the chief corner-stone;
This is the Lord's doing,
And marvellous in our sight.'"

When the high priests and the Pharisees heard these stories, they knew that he was speaking about them, and they wished to seize him but were afraid of the common people who regarded him as a prophet.

JESUS CONDEMNS THOSE
WHO PRETEND TO BE GOOD

The common people were listening to Jesus eagerly. As he taught he said, "Be on your guard against the scribes, who like to walk about in long robes and to have the people bow to them in the market-places. They like to sit in the front seats in the synagogue and in the best places at feasts. These, who use up the property of widows and then to cover their guilt make long prayers, will receive the greater condemnation."

He also said, "Woe to you scribes! For you load men with burdens heavy to bear, which you yourselves do not touch with one of your fingers. Woe to you, scribes and Pharisees, hypocrites! You shut in men's faces the door to the Kingdom of God; for you neither enter yourselves nor let those enter who wish to come in.

"Woe to you, scribes and Pharisees, hypocrites! For you carefully pay to the Temple the tenth part of what grows in your garden, but you do not show justice, mercy, and faithfulness. Blind guides, who strain out the gnat and swallow the camel!

"Woe to you, scribes and Pharisees, hypocrites! For you make clean the outside of the cup and the plate, and then fill them with your greed and selfishness. Blind Pharisee! first make clean the inside of the cup, that the outside as well may become clean.

"Woe to you, scribes and Pharisees, hypocrites! For you are like whitewashed tombs, beautiful outside, but inside full of dead men's bones and filth. So you yourselves appear upright, but inside you are full of hypocrisy and sin."

JESUS WARNS HIS DISCIPLES

As Jesus went out of the Temple, one of his disciples said to him, "Master, see what great stones and what a beautiful building!" Then Jesus answered, "This Temple, made by man's hands, shall be destroyed. But another will soon arise, made without hands." And as he sat on the Mount of Olives opposite the Temple, Peter and James and John and Andrew asked him privately, "Tell us, when shall these things happen, and what is to be the sign to show when all these things are about to happen?"

Jesus said to them, "No one knows the day or the hour when this will happen, not even the angels in heaven, nor the Son, but only the Father."

"The Kingdom of God shall be like ten maidens who took their torches and went out to meet the bridegroom. Five of them were foolish and five were wise. For the foolish ones, when they took their torches, took no oil with them; but the wise took oil in their vessels with their torches.

"Now while the bridegroom delayed, they all slumbered and slept. And at midnight a cry was raised: 'Look! The bridegroom! Come out to meet him!'

Then all those maidens rose, and trimmed their torches. And the foolish ones said to the wise, 'Give us some of your oil; for our torches are going out.' But the wise maidens answered, 'There may not be enough for us and for you. Go rather to those who sell, and buy for yourselves.'
Now while they went away to buy, the bridegroom came and those who were

ready went in with him to the marriage feast; and the door was shut.

Afterward the other maidens came also and said, 'Sir, open to us.' But he answered, 'I tell you truly, I do not know you.'

"Watch, therefore, for you do not know the day nor the hour when the Kingdom of God shall come."

JESUS CURES A BLIND MAN

As Jesus was passing along the road he saw a man who was born blind, and the disciples asked him, "Master, for whose sin, his own or his parents', was this man born blind?" Jesus answered, "Neither for his own sin nor his parents', but that God's power to heal may be shown in him. We must do the work of him who sent me while day lasts; night is coming when no man can work. While I am in the world, I am the light of the world."

When he had said this, he spat on the ground and made clay with the saliva, put the clay on the eyes of the blind man, and said to him, "Go, wash in the Pool of Siloam." So he went off and washed, and returned able to see.

Then the neighbors and those who before had seen him begging said, "Is not this the man who used to sit and beg?" Some said, "It is he." Others said, "No, but he is like him." He said, "I am the man." So they said to him, "How then were your eyes opened?" He answered, "The man who is called Jesus made clay and put it upon my eyes, and said to me, 'Go to the Pool of Siloam and wash.' So I went away and washed, and I received my sight." They asked him, "Where is he?" He answered, "I do not know."

Then they brought the man who had once been blind to the Pharisees. Now it was on the Sabbath that Jesus had made the clay and opened his eyes. Therefore the Pharisees asked him again how he had received his sight, and he told them, "Jesus put clay on my eyes and I washed them and can see." Then some of the Pharisees said, "This man does not come from God, for he does not keep the Sabbath."

Others said, "How can a sinner do such wonderful deeds of healing?" And they could not agree among themselves. So they asked the blind man once more, "What have you to say about him, for it was your eyes that he opened?" The man replied, "He is a prophet."

Now the Jews would not believe that he had been born blind and had received his sight until they called his parents and asked them, "Is this your son who you say was born blind? How is it that he now can see?" His parents answered them, "We know that this is our son and that he was born blind, but we do not know why he can now see nor who opened his eyes. He is of age; ask him, he can speak for himself." His parents said this because they were afraid of the Jews; for the Jews had already agreed that any one who said that Jesus was the Christ should be put out of the synagogue. That was why his parents said, "He is of age, ask him."

So the Jews again called the man who had been born blind, and said to him, "Give God the praise; we know that this man Jesus is a sinner." He answered and said, "I do not know whether he is a sinner; one thing I do know, that, although I was blind, I now see." So they said to him, "What did he do to you? How did he give you your sight?" He replied, "I have told you already, but you would not listen to me. Why do you want to hear it again? Do you also wish to become his disciples?" Then they reviled him and said, "You are his disciple, but we are disciples of Moses. We know that God spoke to Moses, but we do not know where this man came from." The man answered, "This is strange! You do not know where he comes from, and yet he gave me my sight! We know that God does not listen to sinners but that he does listen to him who worships him and does his will. Since the world began no one has ever heard of sight being given to a man born blind. If this man were not from God, he could do nothing." They answered, "You were born wholly bad, and yet you would teach us?" Then they put him out of the synagogue.

Jesus heard that they had put him out, and meeting him said, "Do you believe in the Son of God?" He answered, "Who is he, sir? Tell me that I may believe." Jesus said to him, "Not only have you seen him but he is now talking to you." The man said, "Then I do believe, Master," and he worshipped him, and Jesus said to him, "It is to right wrongs that I have come to this world, that the blind may see and that those who see may become blind." Hearing this, some of the Pharisees who were with him said, "And are we blind?" Jesus replied, "If you were blind you would not be guilty; but you say, 'We can see,' and so your sin remains."

JESUS TELLS WHAT HE CAME TO DO

Jesus said to the people, "I am the light of the world; he who follows me shall not walk in darkness, but shall have the light which gives life."

As Jesus spoke these words many believed in him. Then he said to the Jews who had believed in him, "If you faithfully do what I say, you are truly my disciples, and you shall know the truth and the truth shall set you free."

They answered him, "We are Abraham's descendants and have never been slaves to any man. What do you mean by saying, 'You shall be set free'?"

Jesus answered them, "Truly, I tell you, every one who sins is a slave of sin. The slave does not remain in the household forever, but the Son remains forever. If therefore the Son sets you free, you shall be free indeed.

"I am the Door; if any man enters by me he shall be saved and shall go in and go out and find pasture. The thief comes only to steal and kill and destroy. I have come that they may have life, and that they may have it more abundantly.

"I am the Good Shepherd; the good shepherd lays down his life for the sheep. But a hired man, who is not a shepherd and does not own the sheep, leaves them and runs away when he sees the wolf coming, and the wolf snatches the sheep and scatters them. The hired man runs away because he is only a hired man and does not care for the sheep.

"I am the Good Shepherd and know my own, and my own know me, just as the

Father knows me and I know the Father, and I lay down my life for the sheep. I have other sheep which do not belong to this fold; I must lead them also, and they will hear my voice, and they will be one flock and one shepherd."

JESUS BRINGS LAZARUS BACK TO LIFE

Now a certain man, Lazarus of Bethany, was sick. He was the brother of Martha and of the Mary who anointed the Master with perfume and wiped his feet with her hair. Jesus loved Martha, and her sister, and Lazarus.

So the sisters sent word to him, "Master, he whom you love is sick." But when Jesus heard it he said, "This sickness is not to end in death, but it is for the glory of God, that the Son of God may be glorified by it."

So when he heard that Lazarus was sick, he stayed where he was two days. After that he said to the disciples, "Let us go again into Judea. Our friend Lazarus has fallen asleep, but I am going to waken him." The disciples said to him, "Master, if he has fallen asleep he will get well." Now Jesus had spoken of his death, but they thought that he meant taking rest in sleep. So Jesus said to them plainly, "Lazarus isdead, and for your sakes I am glad that I was not there, so that you may learn to believe. But let us go to him."

When Jesus came he found that Lazarus had been in the tomb four days. Now Bethany was only about two miles from Jerusalem, and many of the Jews had come to comfort Mary and Martha about their brother.

When Martha heard that Jesus was coming, she went out to meet him, while Mary stayed at home. Martha said to Jesus, "Master, if you had been here my brother would not have died, but I know that even now God will give you whatever you ask him." Jesus said to her, "Your brother shall rise again." Martha said to him, "I know that he shall rise again, at the resurrection on the last day." Jesus said to her,

"I am the resurrection and the life. He who believes in me shall live even though he die; and whoever lives and believes in me shall never die. Do you believe this?" She said to him, "Yes, Master, I do believe that you are the Christ, the Son of God who was to come into the world."

When Martha had said this she went away to call Mary, her sister, telling her secretly, "The Master is here and is calling you." When Mary heard this she rose quickly and went to him. Jesus had not yet come into the village but was still in the place where Martha met him. When the Jews who were trying to comfort Mary in the house saw her rise up quickly and go out, they followed her, supposing that she was going to weep at the tomb. But when Mary reached the place where Jesus was and saw him, she fell at his feet, saying to him, "Master, if you had been here, my brother would not have died."

When Jesus saw her and the Jews who came with her weeping, he was deeply moved, and said in great distress, "Where have you laid him?" They said to him, "Master, come and see." Jesus wept. The Jews therefore said, "See how he loved him!" Some of them said, "Could not this man who gave sight to the blind have also kept Lazarus from dying?"

Jesus was again deeply moved, as he came to the tomb. It was a cave, and a stone lay against it. Jesus said, "Take away the stone." Martha, the dead man's sister, said to him, "Master, by this time his body has begun to decay, for he has been dead four days." Jesus said to her, "Did I not tell you that if you only would believe you should see the glory of God?" So they removed the stone, and Jesus lifted up his eyes and said, "Father, I thank thee that thou hast heard me. I knew that thou always dost listen to me, but I spoke for the sake of the people standing near, that they may believe that thou hast sent me." When he had said this, he cried in a loud voice, "Lazarus, come forth." Then he who was dead came forth with his hands and feet wrapped in bandages and his face bound with a cloth. Jesus said to them, "Untie him and let him go."

Then many of the Jews who had come with Mary and had seen what Jesus did, believed in him.

JESUS PRAISES A WOMAN WHO GAVE HER BEST

While Jesus was at dinner at Bethany in the house of Simon, the jar-maker, a woman came in with an alabaster jar of pure perfume, which was very costly. Breaking the jar she poured the perfume over his head.

Some said to each other in indignation, "Why this waste of perfume? It might have been sold for more than three hundred silver pieces and the money given to the poor."

But because they found fault with her, Jesus said, "Let her alone, why do you trouble her? She has done me a beautiful service. The poor are with you always; to them you can do good whenever you wish, but me you will not always have. She has done what she could; she has poured oil on my body beforehand for burial. I tell you, wherever through all the world the good news is told, this deed of hers will be told in memory of her."

JESUS EATS THE LAST SUPPER WITH HIS DISCIPLES

Judas Iscariot, one of the twelve disciples, went to the high priests with the intention of betraying Jesus. And when they heard, they rejoiced, promising to give him money; and he began to look for an opportunity to betray him.

On the first day of the Feast of Unleavened Bread, when the Jews kill the lambs that are sacrificed at the Passover Feast, Jesus' disciples said to him, "Where do you wish us to make ready for your passover meal?"

So Jesus sent two of his disciples, saying to them, "Go into the city, where you will meet a man carrying a jar of water. Follow him and say to the owner of whatever house he enters, 'The Master says, Where is my room in which I may eat the passover meal with my disciples?' He will show you a large upper room already furnished. There make ready for us." So the disciples went into the city and found things as he had said they would; and they prepared for the Passover.

When it was evening Jesus came with his twelve disciples; and while they were eating at the table, he said, "I know surely that one of you now eating with me will betray me." In deep sorrow the disciples said to him, one after the other, "Surely it is not I?" He said to them, "It is one of the twelve, one who is dipping his fingers into the dish with me. The Son of Man will depart as it has been foretold of him, but woe to that man by whom the Son of Man is betrayed! It would be better for that man if he had never been born!"

Then Jesus took the bread and, when he had given thanks to God, he broke it and said, "This is my body which is broken for you; do this in remembrance of me."

In the same way, after he had eaten, Jesus took the cup, and when he had given thanks to God, he gave it to his disciples and they drank of it. Then he said, "This is the new covenant made by my blood which is shed for many. As often as you drink this cup, do it in remembrance of me." Then after singing a hymn they went out to the Mount of Olives.

There Jesus said to them, "You will all desert me, for it is written in the scriptures: 'I will smite the shepherd and the sheep will be scattered.' But after I have risen, I will go before you into Galilee."

Peter said to him, "Though all others should desert you, I will not."

Jesus said to him, "Indeed I tell you, this very night before the cock crows you will deny three times that you know me." But Peter said more emphatically, "Even if I have to die with you, I will never deny you."

And all of them said the same.

JESUS ENCOURAGES HIS FRIENDS AND HELPERS

Jesus said, "Let not your heart be troubled; you believe in God, believe also in me. In my Father's house are many homes; if it were not so, I would have told you, for I go to prepare a place for you. And if I go and prepare a place for you, I will return and take you to be with me that where I am, you may be also; and you know the way to the place where I am going."

Thomas said to him, "Master, we do not know where you are going; how then can we know the way?" Jesus said to him, "I am the way, the truth, and the life; no man comes to the Father except through me. If you had learned to know me, you would have known my Father also; from now on you know him and have seen him."

Philip said to him, "Master, let us see the Father and we will be satisfied." Jesus said to him, "Have I been all this time with you and yet you do not know me, Philip? He who has seen me has seen the Father; then how can you say, 'Let us see the Father'? Do you not believe that I am in the Father and the Father in me? The words that I speak do not come from me but from the Father who lives in me. Believe me, that I am in the Father and the Father in me, or else believe me ecause of the work itself. I say to you, he who believes in me will do the work which I do and still greater works than these, for I go to the Father. And whatever you shall ask in my name I will do, that the Father may be glorified through the Son. If you ask anything in my name, I will do it.

"If you love me you will keep my commands, and I shall ask the Father and he will give you another Helper to be with you forever, even the Spirit of truth.

"In a little while the world will see me no more; but you shall see me, because I live and you shall live also. He who has my commands and obeys them is the one who loves me; and he who loves me will be loved by my Father, and I will love him and will reveal myself to him.

"I have told you all this while I am still with you; but the Helper, the Holy Spirit, whom the Father will send in my name, will teach you everything and remind you of all that I have said to you.

"Peace I leave with you, my own peace I give to you; not as the world gives do I give to you. Let not your heart be troubled nor afraid. You have heard me tell you that I go away and am coming back to you. If you love me you will be glad because I am going to the Father, for the Father is greater than I. I have told you this now, before it takes place, that when it does you may believe.

"I am the true vine and my Father is the vine-dresser. He cuts away each of my branches that does not bear fruit, and cleans every branch that bears fruit so as to make it bear more. You are already clean because of the word which I have spoken to you. Remain united with me and I will remain with you. Just as the branch cannot bear fruit unless it remains united with the vine, neither can you bear fruit unless you remain united with me. I am the vine, you are the branches. He who remains united with me and I with him bears much fruit, but apart from me you can do nothing.

"If you remain united with me and my words remain in you, ask whatever you will and you shall have it. It is by your bearing much fruit and being my true disciples that my Father is glorified. As the Father has loved me, so have I also loved you;

continue in my love. If you keep my commands, you will continue in my love, even as I have kept my Father's commands and continue in his love.

"I have told you all this that my joy may be yours, and that your joy may be complete. This is my command: 'Love one another even as I have loved you.' No man has greater love than that which leads him to lay down his life for his friends. You are my friends if you do whatever I command you. I call you servants no longer, for the servant does not know what his master does; but I call you friends, for I have told you everything that I have heard from my Father. You did not choose me, but I chose you and appointed you to bear fruit that will remain, so that whatever you ask of the Father in my name he will give you."

JESUS IS SEIZED BY THE MOB

When Jesus and his disciples came to a certain place called Gethsemane, he said to them, "Sit here while I pray"; but he took with him Peter and James and John. And as he suffered greatly from deep sorrow, he said to them, "My heart is heavy with sadness. Stay here and watch." Then he went forward a short distance and threw himself on the ground and prayed that if possible he might be spared this agony, saying, "Father, with thee all things are possible. Take away this cup of agony from me. Yet not my will, but thy will be done."

When he came back, he found his disciples asleep; and he said to Peter, "Simon, are you asleep? Could you not watch for one hour? Watch and pray that you may overcome temptation. The spirit indeed is willing, but the body is weak." Again he went away and prayed the same prayer. And when he returned, again he found them asleep, for they were very drowsy; and they did not know what to say to him. Then he came the third time and said to them, "Sleep on now and take your rest. It is enough; the hour has come; already the Son of Man has been betrayed into the hands of wicked men. Rise, let us go; for here is the one who has betrayed me."

While Jesus was still speaking, Judas, one of the Twelve, came up, followed by a mob with swords and clubs, who had come from the high priests and the scribes and the elders. Judas had arranged a signal: "He whom I shall kiss," he said, "is the man. Take him, and lead him away without letting him escape." As soon as he came, he went up to Jesus, saying, "Master," and kissed him. Then they seized Jesus and took him; but one of those who were with him drew his sword, and, striking the servant of the high priest, cut off his ear. Jesus turned and said,

"Have you come out with swords and clubs to seize me as you would a robber? Day after day I have been with you teaching in the Temple, yet you never seized me."

Then Jesus' disciples left him and fled. One young man, however, followed him with only a linen sheet thrown about him; but when the men tried to seize him, he left the linen sheet and fled away naked.

The mob led Jesus away and brought him to the house of the high priest. Peter followed at a distance, and when they had kindled a fire in the middle of the courtyard and sat down together, he too sat down among them. A certain maid, seeing him there by the firelight, looked at him closely and said, "This man also was with him." But he denied it, saying, "Woman, I do not know him." After a little while another person who saw Peter said, "You too are one of them"; but he said, "Man, I am not."

About an hour later another man said, "Certainly this fellow also was with Jesus, for he is a Galilean." But Peter said, "Man, I do not know what you are talking about." Immediately while he was still speaking, the cock crowed. And Jesus turned and looked straight at Peter. Then Peter remembered how the Lord had said to him, "Before the cock crows to-day you will deny me three times." And Peter went out and wept bitterly.

JESUS IN THE HANDS OF HIS ENEMIES

The men who seized Jesus mocked him and flogged him. They also blindfolded him and said, "Prophet, tell us who is it that struck you?"

And they said many other things, insulting him.

At daybreak they brought him before the council at which were gathered the elders, both the chief priests and the scribes. And they tried to get evidence against him to have him put to death, but could not find any, for though many made false statements, they did not agree. Some men stood up and falsely said, "We heard him say, 'I will destroy this temple made by the hands of men and within three days I will build another made without hands.'" But the statements even of these men did not agree.

Then the high priest arose and asked Jesus, "Do you not answer? What about these statements that these men make against you?" But he was silent and made no answer. And the high priest asked him, "Are you the Christ? If you are, tell us." He said to them, "If I tell you, you will not believe, and if I ask you questions, you will not answer me. But after this the Son of Man will be seated at the right hand of God Almighty." Then they all said to him, "Are you then the Son of God?" He replied, "It is as you say; I am." So they said, "What further need have we of evidence? We have heard it from his own lips."

Then all the high priests and scribes rose and brought Jesus before Pilate, and began to accuse him, saying, "We found this man leading our people astray, forbidding them to pay taxes to the Roman emperor, and saying that he himself is

Christ, the King." Pilate asked him, "Are you the King of the Jews?" He answered, "I am." Pilate said to the high priests and the crowd, "I do not find that this man has done anything wrong." But they insisted, saying, "He stirs up the people by teaching through all Judea. He began in Galilee, and now he has come even here." When Pilate heard this he asked whether Jesus was a Galilean, and when he learned that he was and that he came under Herod's rule, he sent him to Herod Antipas, who was also in Jerusalem at this time.

Herod was glad to see Jesus. He had long wished to see him because of what he had heard about him, and because he also hoped to see him do some wonderful deed. Although Herod asked him many questions, Jesus made no answer, and the high priests and the scribes loudly shouted their charges against him. Then Herod, and his soldiers, after mocking him, and dressing him in a bright colored robe, sent him back to Pilate.

Pilate then called together the high priests and other officials and the people, and said, "You brought me this man on the charge that he stirred up the people to rebel. Now I have examined him before you and found no guilt in him of those things of which you accuse him; no, nor has Herod, for he has sent him back to us. You see that he has done nothing that calls for death. I will therefore have him flogged and then release him" (for it was the custom at this feast to release for them one man). But they all cried out, "Away with him and release for us Barabbas" (a man who had been put into prison because of a riot which had occurred in the city, and on the charge of murder). Pilate spoke to them again, because he wished to release Jesus; but still they shouted, "Crucify him! Crucify him!" He said to them for the third time, "Why, what crime has this man committed? I have found no reason to put him to death. I will therefore have him flogged and then release him." But they shouted and demanded that he should be crucified. And so Pilate, wishing to please the people, released Barabbas, but Jesus he turned over to them to be crucified.

JESUS IS CRUCIFIED BY HIS ENEMIES

The soldiers led Jesus to the courtyard of the governor's palace and called together the whole company. Then they clothed him in a purple robe and, making a crown of thorns, they put it on his head and began to salute him, "Hail, King of the Jews!" They struck him on the head with a reed and spat on him, and on bended knee paid homage to him. After they had made sport of him, they stripped off the purple robe and put on his own clothes, and led him out to be crucified.

They forced a man named Simon, of Cyrene, who was coming in from the country, to carry his cross. So they brought Jesus to the place called Golgotha, which means, the place of the skull. And they offered him wine mixed with myrrh, but he would not take it. Then they crucified him and divided his clothes among them, drawing lots to decide what each should take. It was nine in the morning when they crucified him. The inscription over his head stating the charge against him read:

THE KING OF THE JEWS

With him they crucified two robbers, one on his right and one on his left. And those who passed by scoffed at him, shaking their heads in derision and saying, "Ha! you who were to destroy the Temple and rebuild it in three days, save yourself and come down from the cross!"

In the same way the high priests and the scribes mocked him among themselves and said, "He saved others, but he cannot save himself. Let the Christ, the 'King of Israel,' now come down from the cross, that we may see and believe!" But Jesus said, "Father, forgive them, for they know not what they do."

One of the criminals who was crucified also scoffed at him, saying, "Are you not the Christ? Save yourself and us!" But the other said in rebuke, "Have you no fear of God even though you are being put to death? We are suffering justly, receiving what we deserve for our crimes, but he has done no wrong." Then he said, "Jesus, remember me when you enter your kingdom." Jesus said to him, "This very day you will be with me in paradise."

Now beside the cross of Jesus stood his mother. Seeing her and the disciple whom he loved standing near, Jesus said to her, "Woman, he is your son!" And to the disciple he said, "She is your mother!" And from that hour the disciple took her into his own home.

Darkness covered the whole land from noon until three o'clock in the afternoon. At that hour Jesus cried aloud, "Eloi, Eloi, lama sabachthani," which means, "My od, my God, why hast thou forsaken me?"

When they heard it, some who stood by, said, "He is calling Elijah." And a man ran and, soaking a sponge in vinegar, put it on the end of a reed and was about to give it to him to drink when the others said, "Stop, let us see if Elijah will come to take him down." But Jesus uttered a loud cry and gave up his life. And the curtain of the Temple was torn in two from the top to the bottom. When the Roman captain who stood facing him saw in what way he died, he said, "Surely this man was a son of God."

Looking on from a distance were some women also, among them Mary of Magdala, Mary the mother of James, the younger, and of Joses, and Salome, who had followed him and waited on him when he was in Galilee, and many other women who had come up with him to Jerusalem.

Because it was now evening of the day before the Sabbath, Joseph of Arimathæa, an honorable member of the Jewish national council, who was himself looking for the coming of the Kingdom of God, went to Pilate and had the courage to ask him for the body of Jesus. Pilate, surprised that he was dead, called the captain and asked whether Jesus was already dead, and when he learned this from the captain he gave the body to Joseph. After Joseph had taken Jesus from the cross, he wrapped him in a linen sheet which he had bought, and laid him in a tomb cut out ofrock; and he rolled a stone against the door of the tomb. And Mary of Magdala and Mary the mother of Joses, watched to see where Jesus was laid.

JESUS CONQUERS DEATH

When the Sabbath was over, Mary of Magdala, Mary the mother of James, and Salome bought spices to embalm Jesus. Soon after sunrise on the first day of the week they went to the tomb, and they said to one another, "Who will roll away the stone for us from the door?" But they found that the stone, although very large, had been rolled to one side.

On entering the tomb they saw a young man in a white robe sitting on the right, and they trembled and were afraid. But he said to them, "Do not be afraid. You are looking for Jesus of Nazareth, who was crucified. He is risen; he is not here. See the place where he was laid! But go and tell his disciples and Peter, 'He is going before you into Galilee; there you will see him, as he told you.'"

Then they remembered Jesus' words, and returning from the tomb they told these things to the eleven disciples and to all the others; but to them, the story seemed to be nonsense, and they were not believed. Peter, however, ran to the tomb, but when he looked in he saw only the linen bandages; and he went home wondering what had happened.

But Mary of Magdala stood weeping outside the tomb. As she wept, she stooped down and looked into the tomb and saw two angels in white sitting, one at the head and the other at the feet, where the body of Jesus had lain. They said to her, "Woman, why are you weeping?" She said, "Because they have taken away my Master and I do not know where they have laid him!"

When she had said this, she turned around and saw Jesus standing there, but she did not know that it was Jesus. "Woman," said he, "Why are you weeping? For whom are you looking?" Supposing that he was the gardener, she said, "Sir, if you have carried him away, tell me where you have laid him, and I will take him away." Jesus said to her, "Mary!" She turned to him and cried out, "Master!" Jesus said, "Do not touch me, for I have not yet ascended to the Father; but go to my brothers and tell them, 'I am ascending to my Father and to your Father, to my God and your God.'" Mary went to the disciples with the news, "I have seen the Master," and to tell them what he had said to her.

JESUS WALKS AND TALKS WITH TWO OF HIS DISCIPLES

On the same day two of Jesus' disciples were on their way to a village called Emmaus, about seven miles from Jerusalem; and as they talked together about what had happened, Jesus himself drew near and went with them; but their eyes were kept from knowing him.

He said to them, "What are you talking about so earnestly as you walk along?" And they stood still, looking sad, and one of them, named Cleopas, answered, "Are you only a stranger stopping in Jerusalem? Do you not know the things that have happened there within these last few days?" He asked, "What things?" They answered, "Why, about Jesus of Nazareth, who proved himself a prophet, mighty in word and deed before God and all the people, and how our high priests and rulers gave him over to be sentenced to death and had him crucified. But we were hoping that he was the one to save Israel. It is now the third day since these things happened. Yet some of our women who were at the tomb early this morning, amazed us. They told us that they had not found his body but that they had seen a vision of angels who said that he was alive. Then some of those who were with us went to the tomb and found it as the women had said. But him they did not see."

Then Jesus said to them, "O foolish men, so slow of heart to believe in what the prophets have spoken! Was it not necessary for the Christ to suffer and so win his glory?"

When they came to the village to which they were going, he seemed to be going farther on, but they urged him, saying, "Stay with us, for it is almost evening, the day is nearly over." So he went in to stay with them.

As he sat with them at table, he took the bread, blessed it, broke it, and passed it to them. Then their eyes were opened so that they knew him; but he disappeared from their sight. They said to one another, "Did not our hearts glow while he was talking with us on the way!"

At once they started back to Jerusalem, where they found the eleven disciples gathered with their companions, and from them they learned that the Lord had really risen and that he had appeared to Simon. Then they told of their own experience on the road, and how they knew him when he broke the bread.

JESUS GIVES HIS LAST COMMANDS TO HIS HELPERS

While the two disciples were speaking, Jesus himself stood among them. And they were frightened and believed that they saw a ghost; but he said to them, "Why are you so frightened? Why do you doubt? See my hands and my feet, that it is I myself. Touch me and see, for a ghost has not flesh and bones as you see that I have." While they were still unable for very joy and wonder to believe, he said to them, "Have you anything to eat here?" And when they gave him a piece of broiled fish, he ate before them.

Then he said to them, "This is what I told you when I was still with you, that everything written about me in the law of Moses and the prophets and the psalms must be fulfilled." Then he helped them to understand the scriptures, and said, "It is written that the Christ must suffer and on the third day rise from the dead, and that in his name all nations must be called upon to turn from their sins and gain God's forgiveness. You yourselves, beginning at Jerusalem, are to tell men about these things."

Now Thomas, one of the twelve disciples, who was called "The Twin," was not with them when Jesus came. The other disciples told him, "We have seen the Master." But he said to them, "Unless I see the marks of the nails in his hands and put my finger where they were and put my hand in his side, I will not believe."

Eight days later Jesus' disciples were again together, and Thomas was with them. Though the doors were closed, Jesus came and stood among them and said, "Peace be with you." Then he said to Thomas, "Put your finger here and look at my hands, and put your hand here in my side. Do not be a doubter but a believer." Thomas answered him, "My Master and my God!"

Jesus said to him, "You believe because you have seen me? Blessed are those who believe though they have never seen me!"

Later Jesus appeared to his disciples by the Sea of Galilee, and in this way. As Simon Peter, Thomas, Nathanael from Cana in Galilee, and the sons of Zebedee, were together with two other of his disciples, Simon Peter said to them, "I am going fishing." "We will go too," they said, and they set out and went on board the boat; but that night they caught nothing. At daybreak Jesus stood on the beach, though the disciples did not know that it was he.

He said to them, "Children, have you anything to eat?" They answered, "No." And he said, "Throw your net over on the right side of the boat and you will catch something." So they threw over the net, and now they could not haul it in because of the great number of fish. Then the disciple whom Jesus loved said to Peter, "It is the Master." As soon as Simon Peter heard that it was the Master, he put on his fisherman's coat (for he was stripped for his work), and jumped into the water; but the other disciples, being only about one hundred yards from the shore, came in the small boat dragging the net full of fish.

When they landed, they saw a charcoal fire burning, and over it a fish cooking, and some bread. Jesus said to them, "Bring some of the fish that you have just caught." So Simon Peter went aboard the boat and hauled the net ashore filled with large fish; and although there were so many, the net was not torn. Then Jesus said to them, "Come and eat breakfast." Not one of the disciples had courage to ask, "Who are you?"

for they knew that it was the Master. Jesus came and gave them the bread and also the fish. This was the third time he appeared to his disciples after he had risen from the dead.

After breakfast Jesus said to Simon Peter, "Simon, son of John, do you love me more than these?" He said, "Surely, Master, you know I love you." Jesus said to him, "Feed my lambs." Then he asked him a second time, "Simon, son of John, do you love me?" And he answered, "Surely, Master, you know that I love you." Jesus said to him, "Tend my sheep."

Jesus said to him a third time, "Simon, son of John, do you love me with all your heart?" Peter was grieved because Jesus asked a third time, "Do you love me?" And he answered, "Master, you know everything, you know that I love you." Jesus said to him, "Feed my sheep."

And Jesus said to them, "All authority has been given to me in heaven and on earth. Go you, therefore, and make disciples of all the nations, baptizing them in the name of the Father and of the Son and of the Holy Spirit, teaching them to observe all things whatsoever I commanded you; and, lo, I am with you always, even to the end of the world."

Jesus showed his disciples, by many proofs, that he still lived,revealing himself to them during forty days and telling them about the Kingdom of God. When he and his disciples were together he told them not to leave Jerusalem but to wait for what the Father had promised--"the promise," he said, "of which you have heard me speak; for John baptized with water, but before many days have passed you will be baptized with the Holy Spirit."

While they were together they asked him, "Master, is this the time when you are going to restore the rulership to Israel?" Jesus said to them, "It is not for you to know the time or the season which the Father has fixed by his own authority; but you will receive power when the Holy Spirit comes upon you, and you will be my witnesses at Jerusalem, throughout all Judea and Samaria and to every part of the earth."

When he had said this and while they were still looking at him, he was lifted up, and a cloud took him out of their sight. And while they were staring into heaven, as he went up, two men clothed in white stood beside them, who said, "Men of Galilee, why do you stand looking up into heaven? This Jesus, who has been taken from you into heaven, will come back in the same way as you have seen him go."

On the Day of Pentecost, as they were all together, suddenly, there came from heaven a sound like the rushing blast of a mighty wind which filled the whole house where they were seated. And they were filled with the Holy Spirit and began to speak in a strange way and to cry aloud and shout.

When this was reported a crowd gathered, astonished and perplexed, and asked one another, "What can it mean?" Others with a sneer said, "They are full of new wine!"

But Peter, together with the eleven apostles, stood up and addressed them: "Men of Judea and all who live in Jerusalem, understand this and listen to what I say: these men are not drunk as you suppose, for it is only nine in the morning, but this is what was foretold by the prophet Joel:

"'In the last days,' God declared,

'I will pour out my Spirit on all mankind;

Your sons and your daughters shall prophesy,

Your young men shall see visions.

"'And your old men shall dream dreams,

Even upon my slaves and slave-girls

In those days I will pour out my Spirit,

And they shall prophesy.'"

"Men of Israel, hear these words: By the help of lawless men you nailed to the cross and murdered Jesus of Nazareth, a man who was proved to be from God through the deeds of healing and the wonderful acts which God performed by him among you, as you yourselves know. But God released him from the bonds of death and raised him to life, for death could not hold him. Lifted on high at God's right hand and having received from the Father the promised Holy Spirit, he has poured it upon us as you now see and hear. Let the whole nation of Israel know beyond a doubt that God has made this Jesus, whom you crucified, both Lord and Christ."

When they heard this, their conscience troubled them, and they said to Peter and the rest of the apostles, "Brothers, what are we to do?" Peter answered, "Say that you are sorry for your sins, and let each of you be baptized in the name of Jesus Christ, that your sins may be forgiven; then you will receive the gift of the Holy Spirit, for it is promised to you, and to your children, and to all in distant lands, to any and toall whom the Lord our God shall call."

With many other words he warned and urged them to save themselves from this wicked time. So those who believed what he taught were baptized; and on that day about three thousand were added to the brotherhood.